Past Masters
General Editor Keith Thomas

George Eliot

Past Masters

Forthcoming

Rosemary Ashton

George Eliot

Oxford New York

OXFORD UNIVERSITY PRESS

1983

Oxford University Press, Walton Street, Oxford OX2 6DP

London Glasgow New York Toronto
Delhi Bombay Calcutta Madras Karachi
Kuala Lumpur Singapore Hong Kong Tokyo
Nairobi Dar es Salaam Cape Town
Melbourne Auckland

and associates in
Beirut Berlin Ibadan Mexico City Nicosia

Oxford is a trade mark of Oxford University Press

British Library Cataloguing in Publication Data

Ashton, Rosemary
George Eliot.—(Past masters)
1. Eliot, George—Criticism and interpretation
I. Title II. Series
823'.8 PR4688
ISBN 0-19-287627-9
ISBN 0-19-287626-0 Pbk

Library of Congress Cataloging in Publication Data

Ashton, Rosemary, 1947–
George Eliot.
(Past masters)
Bibliography: p.
Includes index.
1. Eliot, George, 1819–1880—Criticism and Interpretation
I. Title. II. Series.
PR4688.A75 1983 823'.8 83–6293
ISBN 0-19-287627-9
ISBN 0-19-287626-0 (pbk.)

Printed in Great Britain by
Cox & Wyman Ltd, Reading

Contents

Abbreviations

All page references to George Eliot's novels are to the Penguin editions. I use the following abbreviations:

AB	*Adam Bede*
DD	*Daniel Deronda*
E	*Essays of George Eliot*, ed. Thomas Pinney (London, 1963)
FH	*Felix Holt, The Radical*
L	*The George Eliot Letters*, ed. Gordon S. Haight, 9 vols. (New Haven and London, 1954–6 and 1978)
M	*Middlemarch*
MF	*The Mill on the Floss*
R	*Romola*
SCL	*Scenes of Clerical Life*
SM	*Silas Marner*

1 Mary Ann Evans and Marian Lewes

I venture to believe that the same causes which exist in my own breast to render novels and romances pernicious have their counterpart in that of every fellow-creature. (L I 23)

So wrote, in 1839, the stern young Puritan Mary Ann Evans to her Evangelical mentor, Maria Lewis. In 1856 she was to embark on her remarkable career as George Eliot, novelist. In 1838, at the age of eighteen, she had written to the same friend about the forthcoming marriage of some acquaintances:

I trust that the expected union may ultimately issue in the spiritual benefit of both parties; for my part when I hear of the marrying and giving in marriage that is constantly being transacted I can only sigh for those who are multiplying earthly ties which though powerful enough to detach their heart and thoughts from heaven, are so brittle as to be liable to be snapped asunder at every breeze . . . I do not deny that there may be many who can partake with a high degree of zest of all the lawful enjoyments the world can offer and yet live in near communion with their God . . . but I confess that in my short experience and narrow sphere of action I have never been able to attain this . . . But I am as usual becoming egotistical, and you by the bye have naughtily encouraged the habit. (L I 6)

In 1854, already a distinguished essayist and editor, a free-thinker yet still a strict moralist (and still liable to accuse herself of 'egotism'), Mary Ann Evans went to live with George Henry Lewes as his wife in everything but the legality, for Lewes was already, indissolubly, married. The two meta-morphoses, into Marian Lewes and George Eliot, are related, for Lewes proved the perfect helpmate for the shy authoress. Moreover, theirs was a union not only of mutual attraction but also of shared beliefs. The basis of their intellectual agreement was a faith not in God, but in humanity.

Mary Ann Evans was born on 22 November 1819 at Arbury Farm, Warwickshire. She was the third child of the second marriage of Robert Evans, manager of the large estates of the Newdigate family. Until her mother died in 1836 Mary Ann went with her sister Christiana first to a school in Nuneaton where she came under the religious influence of Maria Lewis, and then to the Miss Franklins' school in Coventry. After her mother's death and Christiana's marriage in 1837, Mary Ann kept home for her father and her brother Isaac, until Isaac, too, left home to be married in 1841. Though her formal education ended with her assumption of domestic duties, she read widely and had lessons at home in Italian and German from a Coventry language teacher, Joseph Brezzi. She also read, under Miss Lewis's guidance, improving works such as the letters of Hannah More and the life of Wilberforce.

By 1841, however, she was becoming sceptical of Evangelicalism. In May of that year her 'narrow sphere of action', as she termed it, widened to include a group of intellectual friends in Coventry. Charles Bray, a wealthy ribbon manufacturer, his wife Caroline (Cara) and her sister Sara Hennell welcomed Mary Ann into their Unitarian and – in Bray's case – free-thinking circles. Bray was a radical and a philanthropist, advocating universal and unsectarian education, the extension of the franchise, the right of workers to form trade unions and co-operatives and the humane treatment of the insane. In *The Philosophy of Necessity; or, the Law of Consequences as Applicable to Mental, Moral, and Social Science* (1841) Bray expressed his determinist philosophy that men's minds are as subject to fixed and unalterable laws as are the phenomena of the physical world. He found support for his belief in the pseudo-science of phrenology, the theory that there are separate mental faculties, each having an organ and a precise location on the surface of the brain. By studying the external configurations of the cranium, one acquired, according to this theory, a reliable index to the development of the various faculties and thus a guide to the intellectual and moral character of the individual. Though Mary Ann later rejected Bray's crude pseudo-scientific notions, at this time she found his ideas stimulating and liberating. At this time, too, she read *An Inquiry Concerning the Origin of Christianity* (1838) by Bray's brother-in-law, Charles Hennell, who expressed his scepticism of the biblical accounts of miracles and accounted for the life of Jesus in purely historical terms.

Mary Ann's orthodoxy was shaken. In January 1842 she refused to go to church, shocking her father and Miss Lewis. Despite remonstrances from her father and her severe older brother Isaac, Mary Ann continued rebellious. She wrote ruefully to Cara Bray of her 'excommunicated state', and she attempted a written explanation to her father, in which she said she regarded the Jewish and Christian scriptures as 'histories consisting of mingled truth and fiction'. To Sara Hennell she wrote in 1843 of her relief that her soul had been 'liberated from the wretched giant's bed of dogmas on which it has been racked and stretched' (L I 162). Though much later she remembered this time with greater understanding of her father's feelings, and though she wrote in 1868 that 'the bent of my mind is conservative rather than destructive, and that denial has been wrung from me by hard experience – not adopted as a pleasant rebellion', she nevertheless always considered the loss of faith in Christianity as a gain in faith in humanity. Like Dorothea in *Middlemarch*, who also moves painfully out of a narrow Puritan medium, she could have said, 'I have always been finding out my religion since I was a

3

little girl. I used to pray so much – now I hardly ever pray' (M 427). Her aim as a novelist, she wrote in 1868, was

to help my readers in getting a clearer conception and a more active admiration of those vital elements which bind men together and give a higher worthiness to their existence; and also to help them in gradually dissociating these elements from the more transient forms on which an outworn teaching tends to make them dependent. (L IV 472)

If we bear in mind this tolerance towards the narrow doctrines she had rejected, we need not be surprised that her first venture in fiction was entitled *Scenes of Clerical Life* and was widely thought to be the work of an Evangelical clergyman. When, in 1869, she praised Harriet Beecher Stowe for showing 'a thorough comprehension of the mixed moral influence shed on society by dogmatic systems', she was touching on a theme and attitude which the two novelists shared.

But the tolerance came later. Meanwhile, in May 1842, Mary Ann once again accompanied her father to church in order to patch up family relations. But she kept up with the Brays, and through them met Rufa Brabant, daughter of Dr Robert Brabant, who had been Coleridge's doctor. Rufa was translating David Friedrich Strauss's *Das Leben Jesu*, the most thorough critical account of the Gospels yet to appear. In 1844, Rufa, now married to Charles Hennell, gave up the task of translation, and Mary Ann took over. The work lasted two years and caused her many problems, doctrinal, linguistic and emotional. The rationalist movement of the eighteenth century had led to the re-examination of biblical texts and the rejection of their supernatural elements. This work had been done both by Hebrew scholars and theologians like Reimarus and Eichhorn in Germany, and by the sceptical philosopher David Hume in Britain. Strauss carried the process of

examination a step further. As he wrote in his introduction to
The Life of Jesus:

It is not by any means that the whole history of Jesus is to be represented as mythical, but only that every part of it is to be subjected to a
critical examination, to ascertain whether it have not some admixture
of the mythical. The exegesis of the ancient church set out from the
double presupposition: first, that the gospels contained a history, and
secondly, that this history was a supernatural one. Rationalism
rejected the latter of these presuppositions, but only to cling the more
tenaciously to the former, maintaining that these books present
unadulterated, though only natural, history. Science cannot rest
satisfied with this half-measure: the other presupposition must also
be relinquished, and the inquiry must first be made whether in fact,
and to what extent, the ground on which we stand in the gospels is
historical.

Taking every event narrated in the Gospels, Strauss examined
first the supernatural explanations offered by orthodox theologians, then the 'natural' explanations of rationalist thinkers
like Eichhorn. Rejecting both kinds of explanation, he
proffered in each case his own mythical interpretation. Thus,
for example, the annunciation to Zacharias of the forthcoming
birth of John the Baptist can best be explained as a story
borrowed from Hebrew poetry, in which long barrenness and
late childbirth are commonly celebrated:

We stand here upon purely mythical-poetical ground; the only
historical reality which we can hold fast as positive matter of fact
being this: the impression made by John the Baptist, by virtue of his
ministry and his relation to Jesus, was so powerful as to lead to subsequent glorification of his birth in connection with the birth of the
Messiah in the Christian legend.

Though Mary Ann groaned under the labour of translating
the three learned volumes, she acknowledged the importance

of Strauss's and other German critical works on the Bible, and she often defended the German 'philosophic spirit' against ignorant and insular British attacks. Mr Casaubon, the pedant of *Middlemarch*, carries on his lonely effort to find the Key to All Mythologies, but, as Will Ladislaw points out, he knows no German and must therefore lag behind: 'the Germans have taken the lead in historical inquiries, and they laugh at results which are got by groping about in woods with a pocket-compass while they have made good roads' (M 240).

The translation of the *The Life of Jesus* was published, anonymously, by John Chapman in June 1846. It was received with caution and disapproval by the orthodox, but welcomed in radical circles. After Strauss, Mary Ann turned her translating attention, appropriately enough, to an important forerunner of the rationalist movement of the eighteenth century, Spinoza. While nursing her father over many months of painful illness, she translated the *Tractatus Theologico-Politicus* (1670), in which Spinoza scrutinised the biblical accounts of miracles and showed an understanding of the social function of religious myth. On her father's death in 1849 she decided to move to London to pursue a career, but first she allowed the Brays to take her abroad with them. Exhausted by caring for her father during his last painful months – their chief enjoyment together being her reading aloud to him Scott's novels – she chose to stay behind in Geneva for five months when the Brays returned home. She lodged with François D'Albert-Durade, a painter with a physical deformity who may have been a partial model for Philip Wakem in *The Mill on the Floss* and who was to translate several of her novels into French. On her return she went to London to lodge in John Chapman's house in the Strand, and soon became an active member of the radical group of authors who met there. Chapman, whom she had met at the Brays' house in 1848, lived with his older wife and the family's 'governess' in an intermittently stormy *ménage à trois*. Marian Evans, as she now called herself, appears to have fallen for Chapman's personal charms too, for her stay was punctuated by jealous arguments between her and the other two women in the house.

However, her relationship with Chapman soon became a purely friendly and professional one which greatly furthered her career. In 1851 Chapman took over the management of the ailing *Westminster Review*, once the great organ of radical politics and materialist philosophy, which had been set up by Jeremy Bentham and James Mill in 1824 to rival the *Edinburgh* and *Quarterly Reviews* and to further the cause of reform. Marian became Chapman's editorial assistant, and it was she, not he, who showed the critical flair needed to restore the *Review*'s reputation. In the course of her unpaid, unsung work as editor she met all the leading liberals and free-thinkers of the time, among them John Stuart Mill, Harriet Martineau, Herbert Spencer, Thomas Huxley and George Henry Lewes. During her three years of editing she was at the centre of literary London. As Henry James noted when reading her letters in 1885, 'there is something touching in the contrast between such a state of mind [i.e. in the early letters of her pious provincial phase] and that of the woman before whom, at middle age, all the culture of the world unrolled itself, and towards whom fame and fortune and an activity which at the earlier period she would have thought very profane pressed with rapidity'.

In her care the *Review* flourished. She handled contributors and Chapman himself with admirable tact. Early in 1852 she held the ring between the hasty and inefficient Chapman and the touchy author George Combe, phrenologist and writer on education and social reform. While the two men wrangled over the publishing of Combe's pamphlet on prison discipline,

Marian smoothed their tempers, at the same time quietly getting on with the difficult task of reducing Combe's hundred-page pamphlet to thirty-two pages for the *Westminster*, to the satisfaction of both. Combe, who had studied Marian's head in 1851 and pronounced on her 'very large brain', now used his phrenological expertise to rebuke Chapman about his handling of the *Review*:

I would again very respectfully recommend to you to use Miss Evans's tact and judgment as an aid to your own. She has certain organs large in her brain which are not so fully developed in yours, and she will judge more correctly of the influence upon other persons of what you write and do, than you will do yourself. (L VIII 33)

A letter from Combe to his fellow phrenologist Bray in 1854 provides a wry footnote to this correspondence. The student of human nature, on hearing about Miss Evans's departure for Weimar with Lewes, asked Bray if there was a history of insanity in her family, 'for her conduct, with *her* brain, seems to me like morbid mental aberration' (L VIII 129).

Thus phrenologists do not necessarily make the best psychologists, though Bray, writing with benefit of hindsight in his *Autobiography*, noted that 'she was of a most affectionate disposition, always requiring someone to lean upon, preferring what has hitherto been considered the stronger sex, to the other and more impressible. She was not fitted to stand alone.' In 1852 Marian fell unfortunately in love with the philosopher Herbert Spencer. Though her one-sided affection for the natural bachelor caused her pain, she was able occasionally to view her case with clarity and even irony. Thus she wrote to him in July 1852 from her lonely summer lodgings in Broadstairs, whither she half-hoped to entice him:

If you decided that I was not worth coming to see, it would only be of a piece with that generally exasperating perspicacity of yours which will not allow one to humbug you . . . I fancy I should soon be on an equality, in point of sensibility, with the star-fish and sea-egg – perhaps you will wickedly say, I certainly want little of being a *Medusa*. (L VIII 51)

A week later the brave bantering tone gave way to wistfulness:

I want to know if you can assure me that you will not forsake me, that you will always be with me as much as you can and share your thoughts and feelings with me. If you become attached to someone else, then I must die, but until then I could gather courage to work and make life valuable, if only I had you near me. (L VIII 56–7)

She must have received a discouraging reply, for in her next letter she wrote, 'all sorrows sink into insignificance before the one great sorrow – my own miserable imperfections, and any outward hap is welcome if it will only serve to rouse my energies and make me less unworthy of my better self' (L VIII 61). Here already in these letters – and the more remarkably because applied to her own painful case – is something of the breadth of view, the irony, the scientific analysis and the moral understanding which distinguish the novels. Twenty years later she invited the reader of *Middlemarch* to widen his sympathy beyond that readily granted to Dorothea to embrace the unattractive Mr Casaubon:

One morning, some weeks after her arrival at Lowick, Dorothea – but why always Dorothea? Was her point of view the only possible one with regard to this marriage? I protest against all our interest, all our effort at understanding being given to the young skins that look blooming in spite of trouble; for these too will get faded, and will know the older and more eating griefs which we are helping to neglect. In spite of the blinking eyes and white moles objectionable to Celia, and the want of muscular curve which was morally painful to Sir James, Mr Casaubon had an intense consciousness within him, and was spiritually a-hungered like the rest of us. (M 313)

During 1853 Marian Evans was at the same time writing the only work which was to bear her own name, the translation of Ludwig Feuerbach's *Essence of Christianity* (1841), and preparing to spend the rest of her life with G. H. Lewes. Spencer introduced her to Lewes in 1852 and noticed, no doubt with relief, that their friendship soon grew close. Lewes was already a contributor to the *Westminster Review* and had behind him a youthful career markedly different from Marian's. He had written articles on English, French, German and Spanish literature, published two unreadable novels (in imitation of Goethe) and a popular history of philosophy. Married to Agnes Jervis, he co-founded a radical journal, *The Leader*, with Thornton Hunt in March 1850. In April Agnes bore a fifth son, whose father was Thornton Hunt. As he and Agnes had agreed to live by Shelleyan principles of free love, he registered the child as his own. But the marriage did not survive the birth of three more children fathered by Hunt. When Lewes met Marian Evans, he was already living apart from his wife, but unable to divorce her because, as far as the law was concerned, he had condoned her adultery. Marian Evans sacrificed her reputation in the eyes of society at large and, more painfully, in those of her brother and sister when she took her decision to live with Lewes. The complete loss of contact with her older brother Isaac, whom she had adored 'puppy-like' as a child but who was already distant and disapproving because of her denial of Christian faith, was the most painful result of her action. The plot of *The Mill on the Floss*, written six years later, and in particular the presentation of the brother–sister relationship in that novel, reveal her sorrow.

However upsetting to her sense of family ties her decision was, it accorded well enough with her beliefs. True marriage for her was one based on the 'natural law' of the affections rather than on any purely legal bond. Already in 1848 she had written to Charles Bray about Rochester's marriage to his mad wife in *Jane Eyre*, 'All self-sacrifice is good – but one would like it to be in a somewhat nobler cause than that of a diabolical law which chains a man soul and body to a putrefying carcase' (L I 268). And in Feuerbach's *Essence of Christianity* she found persuasive support for this view of marriage. Feuerbach took the findings of the biblical critics, including Strauss, a step further – out of historical critical research into anthropology. The essence of Christianity, he wrote, is really the essence of human feeling, and the only true divinity is 'the divinity of human nature'. Religion, according to him, arose as a result of an urgent imaginative need in man to posit some perfect being. 'Man, by means of the imagination, involuntarily contemplates his inner nature; he represents it as out of himself. The nature of man, of the species – thus working on him through the irresistible power of the imagination, and contemplated as the law of his thought and action – is God.' With Feuerbach's religion of humanity, Marian wrote to Sara Hennell in April 1854, 'I everywhere agree'. As late as 1874 she wrote in a letter that her novels

have for their main bearing a conclusion . . . without which I could not have cared to write any representation of human life – namely, that the fellowship between man and man which has been the principle of development, social and moral, is not dependent on conceptions of what is not man: and that the idea of God, so far as it has been a high spiritual influence, is the ideal of a goodness entirely human (i.e. an exaltation of the human). (L VI 98)

For Feuerbach the perfection of the bonds of fellowship between human beings is marriage: 'Man and woman are the complement of each other, and thus united they first present the species, the perfect man.' In human relationships, particularly those between the sexes, love brings with it attendant duties, which therefore need not be enforced by creed or dogma. Marian Evans acted on this belief, calling herself Mrs Lewes and insisting to puzzled friends like Cara Bray that 'if there be any one subject on which I feel no levity it is that of marriage and the relation of the sexes' (L II 213). In an essay of 1855 she objected to the narrow, morally harmful version of Evangelicalism propounded by the preacher Dr Cumming, in which 'a wife is not to devote herself to her husband out of love to him and a sense of the duties implied by a close relation – she is to be a faithful wife for the glory of God' (E 186).

The Essence of Christianity, translated by Marian Evans, was published by Chapman in July 1854. In the same month she left England for an extended stay in Germany with Lewes, who wanted to collect materials for the life of Goethe he was writing. Charles and Cara Bray and Sara Hennell received the following note, dated 19 July 1854:

Dear Friends – all three

I have only time to say good bye and God bless you. Poste Restante, Weimar for the next six weeks, and afterwards Berlin.

Ever your loving and grateful

Marian.   (L II 166)

The journey to Weimar and Berlin was undertaken primarily to help Lewes with his research for the life of Goethe. Undoubtedly, though, he and Marian found it easier to start their life together away from gossiping London. They clearly found solace in the fact that Weimar – where, after all, Goethe had lived openly with Christiane Vulpius for several years before marrying her – tolerated irregular relationships. They soon met and befriended Liszt and his Russian princess, who, as Marian wrote defensively to Bray, 'is in fact his wife'. In her journal she recorded that 'the Germans, to counterbalance their want of taste and politeness, are at least free from the bigotry and exclusiveness of their more refined cousins'.

These 'more refined cousins', in the shape of the London literary world (for as yet her brother and sister in Warwickshire knew nothing of the liaison), were soon discussing the case. Lewes's well-known unconventionality in the past and Marian's free-thinking in religious matters caused some observers to put the worst construction on the affair. Carlyle, to whom Lewes wrote a letter explaining their position, replied kindly, but noted grimly on the envelope of Lewes's letter: 'G. H. Lewes and "Strong minded Woman" '. No wonder Marian wrote bitterly to Cara Bray on her return in 1855: 'Light and easily broken ties are what I neither desire theoretically nor could live for practically. Women who are satisfied with such ties do *not* act as I have done – they obtain what they desire and are still invited to dinner' (L II 214).

One of George Eliot's finest gifts as a novelist is her ability to render the moral outrage and moral confusion of society when its rules appear to be broken by the individual. Thus when Maggie Tulliver returns after her near-elopement with Stephen Guest in *The Mill on the Floss*, St Ogg's, as the chapter heading goes, 'passes judgment':

It was soon known throughout St Ogg's that Miss Tulliver was come back: she had not, then, eloped in order to be married to Mr Stephen Guest – at all events, Mr Stephen Guest had not married her – which came to the same thing, so far as her culpability was concerned. We judge others according to results; how else? – not knowing the process by which results are arrived at. If Miss Tulliver, after a few months of well-chosen travel, had returned as Mrs Stephen Guest – with a post-marital *trousseau* and all the advantages possessed even by the most unwelcome wife of an only son, public opinion, which at St Ogg's, as elsewhere, always knew what to think, would have judged in strict consistency with those results. Public opinion, in these cases, is always of the feminine gender – not the world, but the world's wife . . .

But the results, we know, were not of a kind to warrant this extenuation of the past. Maggie had returned without a *trousseau*, without a husband – in that degraded and out-cast condition to which error is well known to lead; and the world's wife, with that fine instinct which is given her for the preservation of society, saw at once that Miss Tulliver's conduct had been of the most aggravated kind. (MF 619–20)

There is some barely disguised bitterness here, which George Eliot managed to avoid in similar passages in the later novels (for example, when describing Middlemarch's reaction to the revelations about Bulstrode's sinful past), but even here she shows that wide tolerance of human failings which accompanies her clear-sighted criticism: 'We judge others according to results; how else?'

It was indeed 'the world's wife' who felt outraged by the step she had taken, though it produced also in some of her men friends – John Chapman and Charles Bray, for example, both of whom had mistresses – some hypocritical remarks to more orthodox correspondents. When the Leweses returned from Germany in 1855, only a handful of women friends visited Marian, including the early women's rights agitators Bessie Parkes and Barbara Leigh-Smith. As late as 1869 the visiting American academic Charles Eliot Norton observed that only women 'so emancipée[s] as not to mind what the world says about them' ventured to visit or receive George Eliot. Only after the publication of *Middlemarch* in 1873, which consolidated her reputation as the greatest living novelist, and a moral one at that, did she become fully accepted in society, being deemed fit even to be presented to royalty.

Marian helped Lewes greatly in his work on Goethe. While he went out to interview acquaintances of Goethe still living in Weimar, she translated extracts from his works which Lewes wanted to quote in the *Life*. She was also translating Spinoza's *Ethics*. Goethe, who frequently testified to the importance of the philosopher's thought for his own, exercised, with Spinoza himself, the most far-reaching influence on Marian Lewes. Indeed, the three thinkers who most helped to form her ideas on life, art and the connections between them were Feuerbach, Spinoza and Goethe.

Lewes had had a loose agreement with the publisher Bohn about a translation of Spinoza's *Ethics*. Busy with the Goethe, he handed over the task to Marian, who, as the translator of Strauss and Feuerbach, was well suited to render another philosophical work (this time from Latin) into English. Moreover, she had, as we have seen, already worked on Spinoza. Now she set about translating the moral system of the philosopher whose chief distinction was to embrace determinism while persuasively showing the possibility of – and indeed the necessity for – moral sympathy and social duty. Unfortunately, when the translation was finished, Lewes and Bohn disputed the terms, and the work was never published.

By a succession of proofs Spinoza shows that, in the nature of things, human beings are in a state of 'servitude' to their emotions. Furthermore, though we have reason, it 'cannot check emotions'. But the conclusions we draw from these facts need not be pessimistic, for controlled moral action is not only possible, it is *required*, by our very subservience to our emotions (including selfish emotions): 'No emotion can be checked save by another emotion stronger in checking and contrary to itself, and every one refrains from inflicting evil through fear of incurring a greater evil. By this law society can be held together.' On these grounds Spinoza builds up his doctrine of sympathy, based on his notion of 'clear and distinct ideas'. Though 'we have not complete command over our emotions,' we can exercise our limited power of reason to bring about moral awareness:

An emotion which is a passion ceases to be a passion as soon as we form a clear and distinct idea of it . . . it follows that every one has power of understanding himself and his emotions, if not absolutely at least in part clearly and distinctly, and consequently of bringing it about that he is less passive to them.

Spinoza's language is tentative, presumably because of the contradiction involved in accepting our subservience to emotions while at the same time urging us to overcome them. The contradiction arises inevitably for George Eliot too, when she shows us characters, like Tito Melema in *Romola* and Arthur Donnithorne in *Adam Bede*, who are victims of their selfish emotions, and who yet seem to deserve some moral censure.

Spinoza explains emotion as 'a confused idea' which can be self-contradictory. For example, when someone I hate (hatred being an irrational passion) is in distress I am pleased because I hate him, but also sorry because he is of my species, is like me, and I can enter imaginatively into his feelings. George Eliot asks the readers of her novels to educate their feelings by such imaginative sympathy when she demands our pity for unlike-able Mr Casaubon and Bulstrode in *Middlemarch*, for poor irascible Mr Tulliver in *The Mill on the Floss*, for Mrs Transome in *Felix Holt* and for the proud, selfish Gwendolen Harleth in *Daniel Deronda*. And those characters, like Tito Melema in *Romola*, who remain uneducatedly selfish, unable to imagine the joys and sufferings of others, are examples of moral failure.

Goethe was the creative writer who most fully adopted

Spinoza's difficult moral system. When Spinoza wrote, 'a man who is submissive to his emotions is not in power over himself, but in the hands of fortune to such an extent that he is often constrained, although he may see what is better for him, to follow what is worse', he might have been writing a sketch for Goethe's Faust. 'Der Mensch in seinem dunklen Drange/Ist sich des rechten Weges oft bewusst' ('Man is often aware of the right way even when in the grip of dark passions'), says God in the Prologue in Heaven (*Faust*, Part 1). One of the first articles which Marian Lewes wrote for *The Leader* on her return to London from Germany was a short piece called 'The Morality of *Wilhelm Meister*' (July 1855). No doubt judiciously timed to prepare the way for the publication of Lewes's *Life of Goethe* a few months later, it also contains an important statement of her views on literature, and in particular on the art of novel-writing. Goethe's *Wilhelm Meister's Apprenticeship*, as it was known to English readers in Carlyle's translation of 1824, had been much criticised on grounds of immorality. Marian sees in Goethe the truly moral artist who 'brings us into the presence of living, generous humanity – mixed and erring, and self-deluding . . . he is in no haste to alarm readers into virtue by melodramatic consequences; he quietly follows the stream of fact and of life; and waits patiently for the moral processes of nature as we all do for her material processes' (E 146). Though in her own novels she directs her readers more overtly than Goethe towards objects of sympathy and tolerance, and though in the early novels, at least, she falls into conventional melodramatic climaxes (the child-murder and pardon of Hetty in *Adam Bede* and the tragic flood in *The Mill on the Floss*), she shares Goethe's ability to present mixed and erring human nature so as to elicit our sympathetic interest.

One prevalent sin of novel-writing which she castigates in this essay is the so-called moral *dénouement*, in which rewards and punishments are distributed according to those notions of justice on which the novel-writer would have recommended that the world should be governed if he had been consulted at the creation. The emotion of satisfaction which a reader feels when the villain of the book dies of some hideous disease, or is crushed by a railway train [a reference to the smiling Carker of Dickens's *Dombey and Son*?] is no more essentially moral than the satisfaction which used to be felt in whipping culprits at the cart-tail. So we dismiss the charge of immorality against *Wilhelm Meister*, on these two counts – the absence of moral bias in the mode of narration, and the comfortable issues allowed to questionable actions and questionable characters. (E 145)

It is a most intelligent defence of *Wilhelm Meister*. In her own novels George Eliot worked hard to avoid convenient outcomes. Though in 'Janet's Repentance', one of the *Scenes of Clerical Life*, Janet Dempster's disagreeable husband dies rather providentially, and in *Middlemarch* Dorothea's mismatch with Casaubon is curtailed by his early death, any cheap sensation of relief in the reader is checked by George Eliot's painstaking effort to show the women coming to terms with their burdens and, in Dorothea's case, achieving a sad sympathy for her husband, so that his death causes a real loss of direction for her efforts and duties.

It is in her essays of 1855 and 1856 that we see Marian everywhere applying her philosophical principles to literature. The authoritative voice of the essayist evolves by one of those 'natural laws' of progress she so often invokes into the voice of the narrator in her fiction. Whether she is writing about scriptural criticism, evangelical preaching, the social position of women in France, Tennyson's poetry or even the music of Wagner, her terminology is that of 'development'. With Spinoza, Goethe, Comte, Feuerbach, Spencer, Darwin, Huxley, Marx and others, she accepts in all spheres of human study 'the presence of undeviating law in the material and moral world – of that invariability of sequence which is acknowledged to be the basis of physical science, but which is still perversely ignored in our social organisation, our ethics and our religion' (review of Mackay's *Progress of the Intellect*, 1851). What these authors shared, in their different fields of study, was an experimental, scientific method and a belief in natural laws operating in the relations between physical, mental and social phenomena. Thus while Darwin built up in his *Origin of Species* (1859) a mass of observed biological data to give proofs of the gradual development of all living forms by a continuous process of descent with modification, Auguste Comte, coiner of the term 'sociology', studied the evolution of different stages of civilisation, and Marx based his investigation of modern industrial society on a belief in the inevitable sequence of class revolutions that would logically culminate in the dictatorship of the proletariat. All these writers looked to history to verify their claims, and all of them used the methods and terminology of science. So, too, did Wilhelm Heinrich von Riehl, the German social historian, whose books on the 'natural history of German life' George Eliot reviewed with enthusiasm in 1856:

The views at which he has arrived by this inductive process, he sums up in the term – *social-political-conservatism*; but his conservatism is, we conceive, of a thoroughly philosophical kind. He sees in European society *incarnate history*, and any attempt to disengage it from its historical elements must, he believes, be simply destructive of social vitality. What has grown up historically can only die out historically, by the gradual operation of necessary laws. The external conditions which society has inherited from the past are but the manifestation of inherited internal conditions in the human beings who compose it; the internal conditions and the external are related to each other as the organism and its medium, and development can take place only by the gradual consentaneous development of both. (E 286–7)

Though she gave her whole consent to the optimistic belief in necessary progress in matters physical and moral (the most optimistic expression of which was Comte's belief in the imminent dawning of an age of positivism), like Riehl she clung also to tradition, insisted on the sanctity of the past and expressed her belief in progress often in an almost melancholy way. Thus many of her novels are set in the relatively recent past, the better to point up her belief in progress, while at the same time allowing her to cherish the best in past traditions. She often gives panoramic views of social history, from that of Milby in 'Janet's Repentance' to the survey of the Rhine and the Rhône in *The Mill on the Floss* and the imagined coach ride at the beginning of *Felix Holt*. The tone of these passages is both ironic and nostalgic. Writing of the Austro-Prussian War of 1866, she saw the 'care the Prussians are said to have for the wounded Austrians' as 'one of the proofs one likes to register, that we are slowly, slowly, growing out of barbarism' (L IV 292). In 1869 she remarked, more negatively, 'how slowly the centuries work toward the moral good of men' (L V 31). Like Darwin and Marx, she embraced a determinism which seemed often to be incompatible with optimism. She stated the paradox in biological terms in her essay on 'Liszt, Wagner, and Weimar' (July 1855):

As to melody – who knows? It is just possible that melody, as we conceive it, is only a transitory phase of music . . . We are but in 'the morning of the times', and must learn to think of ourselves as tadpoles unprescient of the future frog. Still the tadpole is limited to tadpole pleasures; and so, in our state of development, we are swayed by melody. (E 103)

The problem is how we can be both 'limited' and 'unprescient' and yet 'learn to think of ourselves' in relation to the future frog. Again, in a scientific metaphor she applies everywhere in her novels, and particularly in *Middlemarch* and *Daniel Deronda*, the organism is determined by its medium, yet it must be possible for an organism (an individual like Dorothea or Daniel) to make changes, however small and gradual, in the medium (like the provincial society of Middlemarch).

In the article on Riehl she moves naturally from a consideration of his view of history and real society to the aspirations and limitations of 'our social novels'. Here she states her belief that art should be 'realistic' and that, in being so, it should teach morality. All her intellectual agreements – with Spinoza's ethics, Feuerbach's anthropology, Spencer's sociology, Lewes's current studies in zoology – come together in her prescription for the novel:

Our social novels profess to represent the people as they are, and the unreality of their representations is a grave evil. The greatest benefit we owe to the artist, whether painter, poet, or novelist, is the extension of our sympathies . . . Art is the nearest thing to life; it is a mode of amplifying experience and extending our contact with our fellow-men beyond the bounds of our personal lot. All the more sacred is the task of the artist when he undertakes to paint the life of the People. (E 270–1)

To use the language of 'development', Marian Lewes was preparing to emerge as George Eliot.

2 The emergence of George Eliot: Dutch realism and English provincial life

The article which Marian wrote for the *Westminster Review* in September 1856, 'Silly Novels by Lady Novelists', has special interest for us, because she began writing her first story immediately after finishing it. Her essay is a witty attack on the 'mere left-handed imbecility' of many contemporary novels, which she classifies under headings such as 'the *mind-and-millinery* species', 'the *oracular* species' and 'the *white neck-cloth* species' (genteel Evangelical tracts in narrative form). In the first kind we have no more than the odd hint that 'the working-day business of the world is somehow being carried on', since our attention is constantly focused on the heroine, 'the ideal woman in feelings, faculties, and flounces'. The oracular novelist pronounces on matters of philosophy and religion from 'false notions of society baked hard'. And the Evangelical writer invariably gives us a young curate with a 'background of well-dressed and wealthy, if not fashionable society; – for Evangelical silliness is as snobbish as any other kind of silliness'. All these subspecies of fiction lack the main requisite of literature, 'genuine observation': 'The real drama of Evangelicalism – and it has abundance of fine drama for any one who has genius enough to discern and reproduce it – lies among the middle and lower classes' (E 318). Accordingly, the first of George Eliot's *Scenes of Clerical Life*, called 'The Sad Fortunes of the Reverend Amos Barton', is set among the lower classes in the Midlands, having as its medium the society, traditions and beliefs Mary Ann Evans grew up with.

Lewes, who was corresponding with the Edinburgh publisher John Blackwood over the publication of his articles on sea anemones in *Blackwood's Magazine*, naturally turned to him with Marian's story in November 1856, claiming that it ranked with *The Vicar of Wakefield* in its 'humour, pathos, vivid presentation and nice observation' and with Jane Austen's novels in its representation of the clergy '*solely* in its *human* and *not at all* in its *theological* aspect'. Mindful of Blackwood's religious orthodoxy, Lewes added, 'the tone throughout will be sympathetic and not at all antagonistic'. Although Blackwood was too judicious to be swayed by Lewes's bold literary comparisons, he wrote back immediately: 'I am happy to say that I think your friend's reminiscences of Clerical Life will do.' He praised the humour and pathos but noticed that there was more description than action in the story. Marian and Lewes were aware of this too. In her journal she wrote:

September 1856 made a new era in my life, for it was then I began to write Fiction. It had always been a vague dream of mine that some time or other I might write a novel, and my shadowy conception of what the novel was to be, varied, of course, from one epoch of my life to another . . . I always thought I was deficient in dramatic power . . . [Lewes] used to say, 'You have wit, description and philosophy – those go a good way towards the production of a novel. It is worth while for you to try the experiment.' (L II 406–7)

George Eliot was to find that her best medium was not the short story but the long panoramic novel, in which she could relate, minutely but unhurriedly, like Goethe and Scott, the private lives of her characters to the public life of which they are a part.

'Amos Barton' opens with some deft scene-painting. In the manner of Scott, whose novels George Eliot revered both for their qualities of tolerance and humour and for their 'sacred' connection with memories of her father, she adopts an urbane tone. Inviting the reader to join her, she reflects on the changes and continuity of life in the village of Shepperton over the last quarter of a century:

Shepperton Church was a very different-looking building five-and-twenty years ago. To be sure, its substantial stone tower looks at you through its intelligent eye, the clock, with the friendly expression of former days; but in everything else what changes! . . . Pass through the baize doors and you will see the nave filled with well-shaped benches, understood to be free seats; while in certain eligible corners, less directly under the fire of the clergyman's eye, there are pews reserved for the Shepperton gentility. Ample galleries are supported on iron pillars, and in one of them stands the crowning glory, the very clasp or aigrette of Shepperton church-adornment – namely an organ, not very much out of repair, on which a collector of small rents differentiated by the force of circumstances into an organist, will accompany the alacrity of your departure after the blessing, by a sacred minuet or an easy 'Gloria'.

Immense improvement! says the well-regulated mind, which unintermittingly rejoices in the New Police, the Tithe Commutation Act, the penny-post, and all guarantees of human advancement, and has no moments when conservative-reforming intellect takes a nap, while imagination does a little Toryism by the sly, revelling in regret that dear, old, brown, crumbling, picturesque inefficiency is everywhere giving place to spick-and-span new-painted, new-varnished efficiency, which will yield endless diagrams, plans, elevations, and sections, but alas! no picture. Mine, I fear, is not a well-regulated mind: it has an occasional tenderness for old abuses; it lingers with a certain fondness over the days of nasal clerks and top-booted parsons, and has a sigh for the departed shades of vulgar errors. (SCL 41–2)

The combination of slightly coy nostalgia and knowing irony, not quite controlled here, presages the more successful philosophical panoramas of society in the later novels. Here, as we would expect in the writer of those remarkable essays of the

1850s, is a commitment – albeit qualified – to a belief in 'human advancement' and a newly current biological term, 'differentiated', applied, with the full force of its meaning, to society.

Perhaps with Charlotte Brontë's *Shirley* (1849) as an encouraging model, George Eliot presents her clergyman from a determinedly down-to-earth point of view. The vocabulary is familar from her translations of Feuerbach and Spinoza: it is that of fellowship, sympathy, imagination. Chapter five begins as follows:

The Rev. Amos Barton, whose sad fortunes I have undertaken to relate, was, you perceive, in no respect an ideal or exceptional character; and perhaps I am doing a bold thing to bespeak your sympathy on behalf of a man who was so very far from remarkable, – a man whose virtues were not heroic, and who had no undetected crime within his breast; who had not the slightest mystery hanging about him, but was palpably and unmistakably commonplace; who was not even in love, but had had that complaint favourably many years ago ... Yet these commonplace people – many of them – bear a conscience, and have felt the sublime prompting to do the painful right; they have their unspoken sorrows, and their sacred joys; their hearts have perhaps gone out towards their first-born, and they have mourned over the irreclaimable dead. Nay, is there not a pathos in their very insignificance – in our comparison of their dim and narrow existence with the glorious possibilities of that human nature which they share?

Depend upon it, you would gain unspeakably if you would learn with me to see some of the poetry and the pathos, the tragedy and the comedy, lying in the experience of a human soul that looks out through dull grey eyes, and that speaks in a voice of quite ordinary tones. (SCL 80–1)

As to the plot, George Eliot finds herself in a difficulty. Committed to 'realism', to the narrating of everyday, unheroic, uneventful lives, she runs the risk of doing without a plot at all. Yet the short-story form demands contraction, so that the crisis, if there is one, comes hard upon the exposition. The result is an imbalance. For the first two-thirds of the work we are being introduced to, and slowly becoming acquainted with, the dramatis personae. The last third of the work paradoxically embraces melodrama, for Amos must be disgraced, his wife Milly must die and Amos must lose his living, all in a short space of telling-time. George Eliot does try to suggest the passing of time within the narrative, but the problem remains. As Blackwood shrewdly observed, 'the windup is perhaps the lamest part of the story'. Nevertheless, it is a remarkable first attempt.

The second story, 'Mr. Gilfil's Love-Story', is less successful. Scarcely a 'scene of clerical life' at all, it embraces, rather surprisingly in view of George Eliot's fictional creed, melodrama and Gothic effects. Much of the plot takes place in a grand manor house; the heroine is a weakly Italian girl, Caterina, unsuccessfully 'transplanted' into English society; there is the obligatory young rake of romantic fiction who toys with her affections. In general, too, pathos predominates over humour. But there are some sure touches of satire and some snatches of dialogue reminiscent of Jane Austen. Blackwood ventured to make some criticisms, but the unknown new novelist 'George Eliot' defended herself stoutly: 'My artistic bent is directed not at all to the presentation of eminently irreproachable characters, but to the presentation of mixed human beings in such a way as to call forth tolerant judgment, pity, and sympathy' (L II 299). Dickens, who received a complimentary copy of the two stories, wrote in January 1858 praising their 'exquisite truth and delicacy' and guessing that the author was a woman.

'Janet's Repentance', the last of the *Scenes*, embodies George

Eliot's religion of humanity. The Evangelical clergyman Mr Tryan comes to the aid of Janet Dempster, married to a drunkard and often tempted into intemperance herself. The narrator observes, 'The tale of the Divine Pity was never yet believed from lips that were not felt to be moved by human pity' (SCL 358). The narrator subjects the small town of Milby to that intelligent scrutiny of human affairs which informs the later novels:

Nevertheless, Evangelicalism had brought into palpable existence and operation in Milby society that idea of duty, that recognition of something to be lived for beyond the mere satisfaction of self, which is to the moral life what the addition of a great central ganglion is to animal life. No man can begin to mould himself on a faith or an idea without rising to a higher order of experience: a principle of subordination, of self-mastery has been introduced into his nature: he is no longer a mere bundle of impressions, desires, and impulses. Whatever might be the weaknesses of the ladies who pruned the luxuriance of their lace and ribbons, cut out garments for the poor, distributed tracts, quoted Scripture, and defined the true Gospel, they had learned this – that there was a divine work to be done in life, a rule of goodness higher than the opinion of their neighbours; and if the notion of a heaven in reserve for themselves was a little too prominent, yet the theory of fitness for that heaven consisted in purity of heart, in Christ-like compassion, in the subduing of selfish desires. (SCL 320)

As Lewes remarked to Blackwood, 'one feels the want of a larger canvas' for George Eliot. She must write a novel.

For *Adam Bede* (1859) George Eliot wisely chose again the Midland social setting in which she grew up. It was at first conceived as another scene of clerical life, again showing a tolerance of religion while quietly dissenting from it. Dinah Morris, the Methodist preacher, most exercises her 'divine' sympathy not in her preaching but in her human kindness to those in trouble. Like Scott in *The Heart of Midlothian*, George Eliot set her novel in the recent past, so that she could combine a genuine, remembered feeling for traditions and sentiments with the historian's philosophical hindsight, his ability to put a past generation into a larger context. Drawing on her memories of her Methodist aunt, Mrs Samuel Evans, on her own juvenile Evangelicalism and her acquaintance with the dialect and customs of Warwickshire, she created a fictional society which was immediately acclaimed for its truth to life. Here is the first evidence of her astonishing gift for creating amusing minor characters, outdoing even Scott and Jane Austen. For example, Mrs Poyser, the wife of a mild tenant farmer, turns the tables on the penny-pinching landlord, Squire Donnithorne:

'Then, sir, if I may speak – as, for all I'm a woman, and there's folks as thinks a woman's fool enough to stan' by an' look on while the men sign her soul away, I've a right to speak, for I make one quarter o' the rent, and save another quarter – I say, if Mr. Thurle's so ready to take farms under you, it's a pity but what he should take this, and see if he likes to live in a house wi' all the plagues o' Egypt in't – wi' the cellar full o' water, and frogs and toads hoppin' up the steps by dozens – and the floors rotten, and the rats and mice gnawing every bit o'cheese, and runnin' over our heads as we lie i' bed till we expect 'em to eat us up alive – as it's a mercy they hanna eat the children long ago. I should like to see if there's another tenant besides Poyser as 'ud put up wi' never having a bit o' repairs done till a place tumbles down – and not then, on'y wi' begging and praying and having to pay half – and being strung up wi' the rent as it's much if he gets enough out o' the land to pay, for all he's put his own money into the ground beforehand. See if you'll get a stranger to lead such a life here as that: a maggot must be born i' the rotten cheese to like it, I reckon. You may run away from my words, sir,' continued Mrs. Poyser, following the old squire beyond the door – for after the first moments of stunned surprise he had got up, and, waving his hand towards her

with a smile, had walked out towards his pony. But it was impossible
for him to get away immediately, for John was walking the pony up
and down the yard, and was some distance from the causeway when
his master beckoned.

'You may run away from my words, sir, and you may go spinnin'
underhand ways o' doing us a mischief, for you've got Old Harry to
your friend, though nobody else is, but I tell you for once as we're not
dumb creatures to be abused and made money on by them as ha' got
the last i' their hands, for want o'knowing how t'undo the tackle. An'
if I'm th' only one as speaks my mind, there's plenty o' the same way
o'thinking i' this parish and the next to't, for your name's no better
than a brimstone match in everybody's nose – if it isna two-three old
folks as you think o' saving your soul by giving 'em a bit o' flannel
and a drop o'porridge. And you may be right i'thinking it'll take but
little to save your soul, for it'll be the smallest savin' y'iver made,
wi'all your scrapin' '. . . (AB 393–4)

George Eliot is able not only to draw such characters for light
comic relief or 'local colour', but also to use them to further the
plot in important ways. Thus it is through Mrs Poyser's sharp
tongue, lashing even the saintly Dinah into tears, that Dinah
admits to herself that she loves Adam Bede. A second such
catalyst is Adam's selfish, complaining mother. Wanting
Dinah to stay and help her after her husband's death, and
seeing in Dinah the perfect daughter-in-law for herself, she
forces Adam into recognising both his own hitherto
unacknowledged love for Dinah and Dinah's love for him:

'Nay but I canna ma' up my mind, when she's just cut out for thee;
an' nought shall ma' me believe as God didna make her an' send her
there o' purpose for thee. What's it sinnify about her bein' a
Methody? It 'ud happen wear out on her wi' marryin'.'

Adam threw himself back in his chair and looked at his mother. He
understood now what she had been aiming at from the beginning of
the conversation . . .

'Mother,' he said, gravely, 'thee 't talking wild. Don't let me hear thee say such things again. It's no good talking o' what can never be. Dinah's not for marrying; she's fixed her heart on a different sort o' life.'

'Very like,' said Lisbeth, impatiently, 'very like she's none for marr'ing, when them as she'd be willin' t' marry wonna ax her. I shouldna ha' been for marr'ing thy feyther if he'd ne'er axed me; an' she's as fond o' thee as e'er I was o' Thias, poor fellow.'

The blood rushed to Adam's face . . . (AB 544)

However, there are some inconsistencies in the novel. In spite of George Eliot's overt claim in chapter seventeen to emulate 'Dutch paintings' in their 'faithful pictures of a monotonous homely existence' – a claim consonant with her views in the Riehl article and her insistence on the commonplace in 'Amos Barton' – the 'Dutch realism' of *Adam Bede* lapses into pastoral idyll, romance, even myth in places. This is partly due to the nature of the catastrophe. Mrs Poyser's niece Hetty is seduced by the squire's grandson, Arthur Donnithorne. She runs away and bears a child, which she murders. George Eliot shows her awareness in a letter to Blackwood of the possible moral objections to the subject. Characteristically she uses the example of Scott to allay his doubts:

The Heart of Midlothian would probably have been thought highly objectionable if a skeleton of the story had been given by a writer whose reputation did not place him above question . . . Yet what girl of twelve was ever injured by the Heart of Midlothian? Of artistic writing it may be said pre-eminently – 'to the pure writer all things are pure'. (L VIII 201)

George Eliot sets the scene of the seduction in a wood; moreover, 'just the sort of wood most haunted by the nymphs: you see their white sunlit limbs gleaming athwart the boughs'.

Hetty 'was borne along by warm zephyrs'; she 'was no more conscious of her limbs than if her childish soul had passed into a water-lily, resting on a liquid bed and warmed by the mid-summer sunbeams' (AB 176). Such passages, though erotically presented, are not easily reconcilable with the 'Dutch realism' of the book. The climax, too, as contemporary critics noticed with dismay, is melodramatic and conventional: a mysterious stranger arrives on horseback with a pardon for the condemned Hetty. As the critic of the *Saturday Review* put it, 'We are taken away from the new region of lifelike carpenters and dairymaids into the hackneyed region of sham legal excitement.' None the less, his annoyance testifies to the success of the novel in winning admiration for its dominant truthfulness.

What George Eliot also does admirably is analyse minutely the psychological drama of conscience in the seducer. Her portrayal of Arthur is the first of many psychological studies founded in her necessitarian but ethical philosophy of action, the Spinozan belief that the individual is the victim of his emotions, but that by getting a clear idea of them he can become less passive to their influence. In a chapter significantly entitled 'Links' she describes how Arthur, meaning to avoid getting deeper into a relationship with Hetty which has begun with some flirting, goes to seek advice from his friend the clergyman, Mr Irwine. By a combination of circumstances, including his own unwillingness to show himself at fault and Mr Irwine's delicate (and lazy) reluctance to pry, George Eliot shows how Arthur misses the opportunity to become aware of the moral danger he is in. Anxious 'not to imply that he came with any special purpose,' Arthur opens the conversation on general topics. Mr Irwine's volume of Aeschylus provides moral matter, and the clergyman comments that 'a man can never do anything at variance with his own nature'.

'Well, but one may be betrayed into doing things by a combination of circumstances, which one might never have done otherwise' [replies Arthur].

'Why, yes, a man can't very well steal a bank-note unless the bank-note lies within convenient reach; but he won't make us think him an honest man because he begins to howl at the bank-note for falling in his way.'

'But surely you don't think a man who struggles against a temptation into which he falls at last as bad as the man who never struggles at all?'

'No, certainly; I pity him in proportion to his struggles, for they foreshadow the inward suffering which is the worst form of Nemesis. Consequences are unpitying. Our deeds carry their terrible consequences, quite apart from any fluctuations that went before – consequences that are hardly ever confined to ourselves. And it is best to fix our minds on that certainty, instead of considering what may be the elements of excuse for us. But I never knew you so inclined for moral discussion, Arthur? Is it some danger of your own that you are considering in this philosophical general way?'

In asking this question, Mr. Irwine pushed his plate away, threw himself back in his chair, and looked straight at Arthur. He really suspected that Arthur wanted to tell him something, and thought of smoothing the way for him by this direct question. But he was mistaken. Brought suddenly and involuntarily to the brink of confession, Arthur shrank back and felt less disposed towards it than ever. The conversation had taken a more serious tone than he had intended – it would quite mislead Irwine – he would imagine there was a deep passion for Hetty, while there was no such thing. He was conscious of colouring, and was annoyed at his boyishness.

'Oh no, no danger', he said as indifferently as he could. 'I don't know that I am more liable to irresolution than other people; only there are little incidents now and then that set one speculating on what might happen in the future.'

Was there a motive at work under this strange reluctance of Arthur's which had a sort of backstairs influence, not admitted to himself? Our mental business is carried on much in the same way as the business of the State: a great deal of hard work is done by agents who are not acknowledged. In a piece of machinery, too, I believe there is often a small unnoticeable wheel which has a great deal to do with the motion of the large obvious ones. (AB 217–18)

Here George Eliot shows that she not only has a philosophical intelligence, but also a creative one. She can embody her moral philosophy in a fictional situation that is 'like life'; she can find practical examples to illustrate her beliefs (Mr Irwine's example of the banknote); and she can frame the situation with her own metaphorical commentary (the 'backstairs influence' of 'our mental business').

The novel was an immediate success with both critics and the buying public. Two thousand copies were sold in the first month, and over thirteen thousand in the first year. Blackwood was the first to praise it; Mrs Carlyle, who received a copy, wrote that she found herself 'in charity with the whole human race' when she had finished it; Spencer, the only friend to be told the secret of Marian's authorship, praised its 'thorough genuineness'; and Mrs Gaskell wrote: 'I have had the greatest compliment paid me I ever had in my life. I have been suspected of having written "Adam Bede".' The only unpleasant note was that struck by the much publicised claim that 'George Eliot' was a Mr Liggins of Warwickshire. The rumour had started after the publication of *Scenes of Clerical Life* and Joseph Liggins, no doubt flattered by the ascription of authorship to him, failed to deny it.

This was an unfortunate result of George Eliot's taking her own county and some of its inhabitants as models for her fictional world. She was reluctant to reveal her identity; so was Blackwood, who now knew it and regretted that her relationship with Lewes could not 'be put straight'. No doubt he also feared a slump in sales and critical acclaim if the secret were revealed. However, it inevitably leaked out. Barbara

Leigh-Smith (now Bodichon) recognised her friend's spirit in *Adam Bede* (though the family in Warwickshire did not); Chapman suspected the truth, and persuaded Spencer to tell him. Marian's natural diffidence about her talents combined with sensitivity about her social position to produce a morbid dislike of all discussion of her work. Blackwood had early on taken Lewes's hint about George Eliot's diffidence, and from now on never wrote critically about her work. He always found something to praise in each batch of manuscripts she sent him, and when he did not like something he merely expressed himself 'puzzled'. It was the right way to deal with her. As she said, Blackwood seemed 'to have been created in pre-established harmony with the organization of a susceptible contributor'.

Her popularity received a slight set-back, as Lewes and Blackwood had feared, when it became generally known in the summer of 1859 that George Eliot was the 'strong-minded' woman living with G. H. Lewes. William Hepworth Dixon jumped to the attack in the *Athenaeum* (July 1859):

It is time to end this pother about the authorship of 'Adam Bede'. The writer is in no sense a 'great unknown'; the tale, if bright in parts, and such as a clever woman with an observant eye and unschooled moral nature might have written, has no great quality of any kind. Long ago we hinted our impression that Mr. Liggins, with his poverty and his pretensions, was a mystification, got up by George Eliot . . .

Even kind Mrs Gaskell wrote, 'I wish you *were* Mrs. Lewes. However that can't be helped, as far as I can see, and one must not judge others.' In fact, George Eliot felt beleaguered on all sides. She complained to Charles Bray that *Adam Bede* was criticised by some for being too tolerant of Christianity. 'Free-thinkers are scarcely wider than the orthodox in this matter,' she wrote, 'they all want to see themselves and their own opinions held up as the true and the lovely.' She continued with a firm statement of her artistic creed:

If Art does not enlarge men's sympathies, it does nothing morally.

I have had heart-cutting experience that opinions are a poor cement between human souls; and the only effect I ardently long to produce by my writings, is that those who read them should be better able to imagine and to feel the pains and the joys of those who differ from themselves in everything but the broad fact of being struggling erring human creatures. (L III 111)

3 Natural history, tragedy and autobiography

George Eliot's next novel, *The Mill on the Floss*, was to produce an uproar among the critics. As early as April 1859 G. H. Lewes wrote to Blackwood that she was writing a new novel, but this time 'of an imaginative and philosophical kind, quite new and piquant'. Blackwood replied that he was keen to have the new work. For once, however, his tact deserted him, and he suggested publishing the work in parts in *Blackwood's Magazine*, without the author's name, remarking that 'it would be great fun to watch the speculations as to the author's life'. He nearly lost his author on this occasion. Her sensitivity, combined with Lewes's sharp business attitude and the tempting offers coming from other publishers, including Dickens in his capacity as editor of *All the Year Round*, led to a coolness between her and Blackwood. But by his efforts good relations were restored, and *The Mill on the Floss* was published, not in the magazine but in three volumes, in April 1860.

Following on the success of *Adam Bede*, George Eliot's second novel sold six thousand copies in the first seven weeks. However, the critics' reaction was less favourable. Lewes blamed this partly on the disclosure of the author's identity, but the novel itself presented problems to critics who were not able to feel the imaginative sympathy it was George Eliot's avowed intention to nurture in them. For one thing, the rural charm and 'religious flavour' of *Adam Bede* were lacking. Although Maggie Tulliver passes through a religious phase, full of renunciation and the reading of improving spiritual works, George Eliot makes it clear that this *is* only a phase, through which Maggie must pass on her way to adulthood. Secondly, when Maggie reaches maturity, she commits an indiscretion which critics hastened to call 'immoral'. The problem is made more complex by the fact that George Eliot is not in full imaginative control throughout the book.

All her works are, in some sense, autobiographical, in that they contain imaginatively wrought creations which exemplify her beliefs, often in settings borrowed from her experience of life in Warwickshire earlier in the century. *The Mill on the Floss*, too, is set among the farming and trading families of the Midlands. But the more particular autobiographical components of *The Mill on the Floss* – the transmutation of Marian Evans's broken-off relationship with her brother Isaac and George Eliot's continuing partnership with Lewes – have a present painfulness for the writer. They are not examples of 'emotion recollected in tranquillity', though George Eliot tries to adopt a Wordsworthian serenity in parts of the novel. She was not able to take consistently the lofty generous view which she admired in Goethe's works (all self-confessed 'fragments of a great confession') and which she herself had achieved towards Evangelicalism in her first works. When her erstwhile Genevan landlord, François D'Albert-Durade, wrote of his surprise at her tolerance of religion in *Adam Bede*, she reminded him that when he had known her in 1850 she had 'not yet lost the attitude of antagonism which belongs to the renunciation of *any* belief'. Writing *Adam Bede* nearly ten years later, she had no longer 'any antagonism towards any faith in which human sorrow and human longing for purity have expressed themselves; on the contrary, I have a sympathy with it that predominates over all argumentative tendencies' (L III 231). The same could not be true of her feelings about her brother.

Marian had not told Isaac of her liaison with Lewes until nearly three years after it began. The fact that she first broke the news to him in June 1857, after the first two *Scenes of Clerical Life* by 'George Eliot' had been published, seems significant. Instead of replying, Isaac got his solicitor to answer on his behalf, saying 'he is so much hurt at your not having previously made some communication to him as to your intention and prospects that he cannot make up his mind to write, feeling that he could not do so in a Brotherly Spirit'. When George Eliot further wrote that 'our marriage is not a legal one, though it is regarded by us both as a sacred bond', the silence from Isaac became total. George Eliot clearly took a little proud comfort, however, from announcing that she was independent financially, having become 'a writer'.

The handling of the 'brother and sister' theme in the novel presents problems. Although, as her contemporary critics quickly saw, George Eliot gives us 'real' children rather than the impossible paragons which appear in some of Dickens's novels, there remains an imbalance in her portrayal of Maggie and Tom. She had written to Sara Hennell in 1844, 'Childhood is only the beautiful and happy time in contemplation and retrospect – to the child it is full of deep sorrows, the meaning of which is unknown' (L I 173). In the novel she shows in several scenes described with dramatic power and gentle humour how stormy the relationship between the children is, made up of 'puppy-like' adoration and fear on Maggie's part and obstinate, boyish punitiveness on Tom's. Yet she appears to endorse, as *narrator*, the view of childhood as a happy time. She ends Book Two, apparently without irony:

They had gone forth together into their new life of sorrow, and they would never more see the sunshine undimmed by remembered cares. They had entered the thorny wilderness, and the golden gates of their childhood had forever closed behind them. (MF 270)

There is, moreover, some awkward narrative caressing of 'poor Maggie' in her great 'need of being loved' and her emergence from tomboyish childhood to that beautiful and noble womanhood which George Eliot had ridiculed in 'Silly Novels by Lady Novelists'. And although she asks us to share her sympathy with hard, unbending Tom in the family tragedy which thrusts adult responsibility on him so young, she has previously made us feel so much *with* Maggie *against* Tom that we are reluctant to extend our full sympathy. Horrified at the critics' dislike of Tom, George Eliot complained to Blackwood's brother and partner, Major William Blackwood, 'Tom is painted with as much love and pity as Maggie.' Yet so close is she to the material of the book that in her delineation of the brother–sister relationship she tends to round off her paragraphs of 'impartial' insight into the opposed feelings of Tom and Maggie with some such final bitter criticism of Tom as this: 'Still, he was very fond of his sister, and meant always to take care of her, make her his housekeeper, and punish her when she did wrong' (MF 92). However unaware George Eliot may have been of the punitive attitude towards Tom which emerges from such narrative interpolations, that attitude, inseparable from a sense of thwarted love and talents on Maggie's part, is one of the dramatic strengths of the book. The childhood scenes are both lovingly and bitterly rendered by one who had experienced Maggie's sense of injustice at the hands of a beloved brother. A fishing expedition, the sharing of a jam puff, the care and neglect of family pets – such everyday childish events carry a weight of passion and complexity which every reader recognises in general terms from his own childhood and at the same time marvels at for the intensity of its detailed rendering in *The Mill on the Floss*.

The personal interest which the brother–sister theme had

for George Eliot led her into structural difficulties. Richard Holt Hutton, one of her best contemporary critics, spoke for many readers when he described the novel as 'a masterly fragment of fictitious biography in two volumes, followed by a second-rate one-volume novel'. George Eliot herself admitted to Blackwood that 'the tragedy is not adequately prepared' because the 'epic breadth' into which she was 'beguiled by love of my subject in the first two volumes, caused a want of proportionate fullness in the treatment of the third' (L III 317). In fact, she does prepare for the famous catastrophe, in which Maggie and Tom are drowned in the flooded river, both by means of 'natural history' and by introducing the idea of the tragedy (as well as comedy) of ordinary lives. She compares Mr Tulliver's lot with that of Oedipus in its combination of character flaw (in this case irascibility and a tendency to litigation) and 'external fact'. 'The pride and obstinacy of millers and other insignificant people, whom you pass unnoticingly on the road every day, have their tragedy too, but it is of that unwept, hidden sort, that goes on from generation to generation and leaves no record' (MF 275). Indeed she succeeds magnificently in gaining our assent for this view of tragedy, particularly as she applies her scientific metaphors to the description of the unconscious part played in Mr Tulliver's downfall by his good-natured, foolish wife:

Mrs Tulliver had lived thirteen years with her husband, yet she retained in all the freshness of her early married life a facility of saying things which drove him in the opposite direction to the one she desired. Some minds are wonderful for keeping their bloom in this way, as a patriarchal goldfish apparently retains to the last its youthful illusion that it can swim in a straight line beyond the encircling glass. Mrs Tulliver was an amiable fish of this kind, and after running her head against the same resisting medium for thirteen years would go at it again to-day with undulled alacrity. (MF 134)

This is an example of George Eliot's ability to adapt the dramatic irony of classical tragedy to the events of everyday life, of 'the working-day world', as George Eliot would say. But the coming of the flood, and its finding Maggie in a boat drifting purposefully (as it were) down the swollen river to find her brother in order to drown embracing him, is tragedy of a different, more melodramatic order. Even here, though, George Eliot is boldly attempting a linking of the realism of 'natural history' and the symbolic, romance element of tragedy. Just as she had remarked on seeing Nuremberg in 1858, '*There* one sees a real mediaeval town, which has grown up with the life of a community as much as the shell of a nautilus has grown with the life of the animal,' so she views, as natural historian, the town of St Ogg's:

> It is one of those old, old towns, which impress one as a continua-tion and outgrowth of nature as much as the nests of the bower birds or the winding galleries of the white ants: a town which carries the traces of its long growth and history, like a millennial tree, and has sprung up and developed in the same spot between the river and the low hill from the time when the Roman legions turned their backs on it from the camp on the hill-side, and the long-haired sea-kings came up the river and looked with fierce, eager eyes at the fatness of the land. It is a town 'familiar with forgotten years'. (MF 181)

From history, the narrator delves even further back to the legend of St Ogg ferrying the Virgin Mary across the river. With her strict historical view of myth, George Eliot adds, 'This legend, one sees, reflects from a far-off time the visita-tion of the floods.' In a sense, the very linking of history and legend here, in accordance with her philosophical beliefs, makes it difficult for her to embrace the purely legendary mode satisfactorily at the end of the book.

Finally, there is the nature of Maggie's 'mistake', her apparent elopement with Stephen Guest. This drew howls of rage from contemporary critics, interestingly catching them in inconsistencies. They could not decide whether they most objected to the probability of Maggie's sexual temptation or its improbability. (George Eliot, anticipating such confusion in response to *Daniel Deronda*, appended an apt motto to chapter forty-one of that novel, from Aristotle's *Poetics*: 'This, too, is probable, according to that saying of Agathon: "It is a part of probability that many improbable things will happen." ') Further, part of the objection was to the weak characterisation of Stephen Guest. How could the noble Maggie fall for such a 'hairdresser's block', as Leslie Stephen called him? Leaving aside the question of Stephen Guest's credibility, what, we may ask, are the terms in which George Eliot writes of Maggie's moral dilemma? Love and Duty are the two 'claims' which she shows at variance here. In her essay on 'The *Antigone* and its Moral' in 1856 she had written that tragedy arises pre-eminently from the 'antagonism between valid claims'. Maggie is temporarily beguiled by her instinctive attraction to Stephen. He represents the claim of 'the laws of attraction'. On reflection, Maggie insists on the counter-claim of prior duties, in this case to Tom, to Philip who loves her and to Lucy, who is engaged to Stephen. George Eliot, like Goethe, from whose novel (known in the English translation as *Elective Affinities*) she borrows the drifting in a boat for the sexual temptation, as well as the term 'the laws of attraction', bravely allows to both claims their validity. Stephen says:

'We have proved that it was impossible to keep our resolutions. We have proved that the feeling which draws us towards each other is too strong to be overcome. That natural law surmounts every other, – we can't help what it clashes with.'

'It is not so, Stephen – I'm quite sure that is wrong. I have tried to think it again and again – but I see, if we judged in that way, there would be a warrant for all treachery and cruelty – we should justify breaking the most sacred ties that can ever be formed on earth. If the past is not to bind us, where can duty lie? We should have no law but the inclination of the moment.' (MF 601–2)

George Eliot goes further, invoking, as she says, the aid of the casuists in deciding moral issues. There is, she asserts, 'no master key' to fit all cases in 'the shifting relation of passion and duty'; we must take into account the 'special circumstances that mark the individual lot' (MF 627–8).

Nevertheless, there is a failure of nerve, which must be related to George Eliot's sensitivity about her own closest relationships. She does not allow Maggie either to marry Stephen, thus admitting his claim (and awarding a prize to Maggie which was not available to the author herself), or to come back and face alone a life of social ostracism – for, as we saw in chapter one, St Ogg's believes her guilty of fulfilled elopement. She had praised Goethe for showing in *Wilhelm Meister* 'large tolerance' rather than obtrusive moralising in depicting 'irregular relations in all the charms they really have for human nature', for 'patiently [waiting] for the moral processes of nature as we all do for her material processes'. The denouement of *Elective Affinities* had been the subject of conversation with Professor Stahr in Berlin in 1854. 'This dénouement, he said, was "unvernunftig" [unreasonable]. So, I said, were dénouements in real life very frequently: Goethe had given the dénouement which would naturally follow from the characters of the respective actors' (journal for 1854). Yet, while intellectually assigning in *The Mill on the Floss* the same imperativeness to the 'natural law' of sexual attraction as to that of the duty to past ties and affections, George Eliot gives less weight to it in the climax of her novel. The theme of love and duty occurs again and again in her work from now on: we meet it in *Silas Marner, Romola, The Spanish Gypsy, Middlemarch* and *Daniel Deronda*. And though she never allows passion to predominate over duty without ensuing tragedy, nor does she take the congenial way out of exalting duty above love. When D'Albert-Durade, who translated *The Mill on the Floss* into French, suggested 'Amour et Devoir' as a title, she wrote back vehemently that he must 'resist to the death anything of the same genre as "Amour et Devoir" ' (L IV 69). Her repugnance may have sprung partly from her constant fear of moralising too much, of 'lapsing from the picture to the diagram' (L IV 300). It is also worth noting that all her novels are named after people or places. This reinforces our sense that she saw her task as primarily that of the descriptive natural historian rather than the schematic moralist.

George Eliot reacted, rather as Tennyson did, with ambivalence to Darwin's culminating work in the field of development, *On the Origin of Species* (1859). She read it while writing *The Mill on the Floss*, and hailed its appearance in a letter to Barbara Bodichon:

It will have a great effect in the scientific world, causing a thorough and open discussion of a question about which people have hitherto felt timid. So the world gets on step by step towards brave clearness and honesty! But to me the Development theory and all other explanations of processes by which things came to be, produce a feeble impression compared with the mystery that lies under the processes. (L III 227)

Some years later, in 1867, she pointed out again the qualifications she always made in her adherence to the principle of development: 'Natural selection is not always good, and depends (see Darwin) on many caprices of very foolish animals' (L IV 377). And her philosophical description of the Dodsons and Tullivers in Book Four of *The Mill on the Floss* exhibits in its bewildering turns of tone and metaphor the melancholy which tempered optimism in her view of historical processes. She begins with the fabled Rhine and the ordinary Rhône:

Therefore it is that these Rhine castles thrill me with a sense of poetry: they belong to the grand historic life of humanity, and raise up for me the vision of an epoch. But these dead-tinted, hollow-eyed, angular skeletons of villages on the Rhône, oppress me with the feeling that human life – very much of it – is a narrow, ugly, grovelling existence, which even calamity does not elevate, but rather tends to exhibit in all its bare vulgarity of conception; and I have a cruel conviction that the lives these ruins are the traces of were part of a gross sum of obscure vitality, that will be swept into the same oblivion with the generations of ants and beavers.

Perhaps something akin to this oppressive feeling may have weighed upon you in watching this old-fashioned family life on the banks of the Floss, which even sorrow hardly suffices to lift above the level of the tragi-comic. It is a sordid life, you say, this of the Tullivers and Dodsons . . . Here, one has conventionally worldly notions and habits without instruction and without polish – surely the most prosaic form of human life: proud respectability in a gig of unfashionable build: worldliness without side-dishes . . .

I share with you this sense of oppressive narrowness; but it is necessary that we should feel it, if we care to understand how it acted on the lives of Tom and Maggie – how it has acted on young natures in many generations, that in the onward tendency of human things have risen above the mental level of the generation before them, to which they have been nevertheless tied by the strongest fibres of their hearts. The suffering, whether of martyr or victim, which belongs to every historical advance of mankind, is represented in this way in every town and by hundreds of obscure hearths: and we need not shrink from this comparison of small things with great; for does not science tell us that its highest striving is after the ascertainment of a unity which shall bind the smallest things with the greatest? In natural science, I have understood, there is nothing petty to the mind that has a large vision of relations, and to which every single object suggests a vast sum of conditions. It is surely the same with the observation of human life. (MF 362–3)

According to the 'onward tendency of human things', Maggie and (less believably) Tom are examples of a younger generation which achieves a 'higher culture' but in so doing 'comes into collision with the older', as George Eliot explained to Emily Davies in 1869. It is characteristic of George Eliot that her head should be with the idea of advancement, while her heart was always at least partly with the stage left behind. Thus she could see, in *Adam Bede*, Nature as 'that great tragic dramatist' of family relations who 'knits us together by bone and muscle, and divides us by a subtler web of our brains; blends yearning and repulsion; and ties us by our heart-strings to the beings that jar us at every movement' (AB 83–4). *The Mill on the Floss* presents the most striking example from among George Eliot's novels of an irreconcilable clash between intellectual optimism about the progress of society – of 'humanity' in general – and a melancholy perception of the sadness, futility, even tragedy experienced by individuals caught in the onward march of history.

4 Wordsworthian fable and historical romance

Now known and widely admired as the great novelist of English provincial life, particularly in *Adam Bede* but also in the first two volumes – the non-controversial part – of *The Mill on the Floss*, George Eliot began to think about a change of direction. As soon as she had sent off the final proofs of *The Mill on the Floss* to Blackwood in 1860, she and Lewes made a journey to Italy. In Florence, Lewes suggested that she try 'a historical romance – scene, Florence – period, the close of the fifteenth century, which was marked by Savonarola's career and martyrdom'. The work for this novel, *Romola*, was to take three years. Meanwhile, as George Eliot wrote to Blackwood in January 1861, 'I am writing a story which came *across* my other plans by a sudden inspiration' (L III 371). This was *Silas Marner*, another novel of English life, but different in plan from the panoramic natural histories of the others. *Silas Marner* is brief and tightly structured, making full use, like *The Winter's Tale*, of a sixteen-year gap to condense both plot and symbolism. It is a moral fable of the nemesis of character and the regenerative influence of a child. As George Eliot wrote to Blackwood:

I should not have believed that any one would have been interested in it but myself (since William Wordsworth is dead) if Mr. Lewes had not been strongly arrested by it. But I hope you will not find it at all a sad story, as a whole, since it sets – or is intended to set – in a strong light the remedial influences of pure, natural human relations. The Nemesis is a very mild one. I have felt all through as if the story would have lent itself best to metrical rather than prose fiction, especially in all that relates to the psychology of Silas; except that, under that treatment, there could not be an equal play of humour. It came to me first of all, quite suddenly, as a sort of legendary tale, suggested by my recollection of having once, in early childhood, seen a linen-weaver with a bag on his back; but, as my mind dwelt on the subject, I became inclined to a more realistic treatment. (L III 382)

The Wordsworthian influence merges, in the simple progress of the plot, with that of Feuerbach's religion of humanity. Silas Marner, the embittered and lonely weaver, loses his gold and finds a golden-haired child, Eppie; the child forces him to forge links with the community and re-establishes his contact with external nature; she 'warmed him into joy because *she* had joy' (SM 184). Though Silas has lost his religious belief, he submits to the dominant religion of Raveloe – a mixture of primitive superstition and kind practical wisdom – for the child's sake. He has her baptised to please his neighbours and to 'do the right thing'. The significance of the event is not, however, primarily religious, but human: by it Silas shares in the human fellowship of the community. George Eliot's treatment is unusually optimistic:

In old days there were angels who came and took men by the hand and led them away from the city of destruction. We see no white-winged angels now. But yet men are led away from threatening destruction: a hand is put into theirs, which leads them forth gently towards a calm and bright land, so that they look no more backward; and the hand may be a little child's. (SM 190–1)

The fact that no agent is assigned to the action of leading men away from destruction suggests that the optimism is rather forced, being a necessary part of George Eliot's mild, Wordsworthian plan (in which a benevolent external Nature may be the agent of human regeneration), rather than fully endorsed by her.

The nemesis to which she refers in her letter to Blackwood is that which befalls Godfrey Cass, son of the squire, who by secretly marrying a girl beneath him in rank has sown the seed which 'by orderly sequence brings forth a seed after its kind' (SM 127). Eppie is Godfrey's child by his imprudent marriage; he takes care not to own up to the relationship, thus clearing a path towards possible marriage with Nancy Lammeter, but also denying himself the opportunity of rearing and loving Eppie. Godfrey's 'moral cowardice' is deftly sketched early in the novel:

The results of confession were not contingent, they were certain; whereas betrayal was not certain. From the near vision of that certainty he fell back on suspense and vacillation with a sense of repose. The disinherited son of a small squire, equally disinclined to dig and to beg, was almost as helpless as an uprooted tree, which, by the favour of earth and sky, has grown to a handsome bulk on the spot where it first shot upward. . . . he would rather trust to casualties than to his own resolve – rather go on sitting at the feast and sipping the wine he loved, though with the sword hanging over him and terror in his heart, than rush away into the cold darkness where there was no pleasure left. (SM 77)

Godfrey's 'god' – 'Favourable Chance' – appears to smile on him: the abandoned opium-addicted wife dies. But Godfrey's relief at not being found out becomes saddened as the years pass and he watches his daughter Eppie grow up happy with her adopted father, while his marriage with Nancy produces no children. Nemesis, gold-symbolism and plot proceed in step, so that just when Silas's gold is found, he is threatened with the corresponding loss of golden-haired Eppie. But the tale is 'regenerative'. Eppie's true affections are for Silas, and she refuses to be adopted by Godfrey. It is a neat, rather uncharacteristic work by George Eliot, except in the link between character and action, and in the idea of the nemesis of conscience which she sketches here in Godfrey Cass.

After *Silas Marner*, which sold well and was praised by critics – though more for the comic scenes among the local worthies at the Rainbow Inn than for its other qualities – George Eliot returned to her studies of Renaissance Florence. As Lewes told Blackwood in October 1861, 'Mrs. Lewes is very well and buried in musty old antiquities, which she will have to vivify.' All her novels so far had been set in the past, and for all of them she researched meticulously, filling her notebooks with facts about politics, fashion, the weather and many other topics in the chosen era. But she had never written about a society more than sixty years back, or outside rural England. Her work for *Romola* was prodigious. Lewes, foreseeing a problem in her ability to 'vivify' the antiquities, warned Blackwood before a visit: 'When you see her, mind your care is to discountenance the idea of a Romance being the product of an Encyclopaedia.' In the event, Blackwood did not publish the novel. George Smith offered George Eliot a magnificent £10,000 to publish it in serial form in the *Cornhill Magazine*. Blackwood was gentlemanly about the defection, and too cautious to try to outdo Smith's terms. *Romola*, in fact, made Smith a loss, and George Eliot subsequently returned to Blackwood for good.

George Eliot was aware of the risk she was taking in abandoning the material of which she was the universally acknowledged master. She wrote defensively to Sara Hennell in 1862:

Of necessity, the book is addressed to fewer readers than my previous works, and I myself have never expected – I might say intended – that the book should be as 'popular' in the same sense as the others. If one is to have freedom to write out one's own varying unfolding self, and not be a machine always grinding out the same material or spinning the same sort of web, one cannot always write for the same public. (L IV 49)

No doubt the subject of fifteenth-century Florence, with its political, intellectual and religious clashes between the 'medieval' and the emergent 'modern' consciousness, seemed to her to offer a new opportunity to study the progress of history. If any of her works may be called 'positivist', it is *Romola*.

Auguste Comte was the founder of the positivist system of social philosophy, which entailed a belief in successive stages of thought and investigation bringing about a progressive increase in knowledge. Indeed, Comte provided a historical account of society which matched Feuerbach's account of religious belief. He divided human history into three epochs: the theological, the metaphysical and the positivist. The close study of the relations between men must now proceed on a scientific basis, since the formal religious basis of social action which had prevailed in the theological epoch – illustrated by the Middle Ages under Catholicism – had been undermined by the metaphysical stage of civilisation, beginning with the Reformation and culminating in the rationalist philosophical systems of the eighteenth century. This latter phase was a negative, destructive one, regrettable but necessary as an interim period of human development. In this view Comte was close to Hegel, Coleridge, Carlyle and others who criticised the prevailing scepticism of eighteenth-century thought, but saw it as a necessary forerunner to a more spiritual age. But Comte went further. There was to be a new faith called positivism, replacing the negative tendencies of the metaphysical era, and it was to be based on scientific observations of the relations between all the phenomena which made up society. As befitted the new industrial age, a scientific, industrial élite was to take over from the priesthood the role of guardians of society. Women were to have a special function in bringing about the positive era. 'Woman', wrote Comte, 'is the spontaneous priestess of Humanity.'

George Eliot's attitude to Comte has long been a subject of dispute. She wrote no essays on positivism, and her references to the system are brief and often ambivalent. In a notebook entry dating from the 1870s she objected, like Lewes, Mill, Spencer, and most other English admirers of Comte, to his advocacy in the *Politique positive* of a new secular priesthood. 'Doctrine,' she wrote, 'no matter of what sort, is liable to putrefy when kept in close chambers to be dispensed according to the will of men authorised to hold the keys.' But she was reading the earlier *Philosophie positive* while working on *Romola* in 1861, and wrote to Sara Hennell that she found Comte's survey of the Middle Ages 'full of luminous ideas'. It was Spencer's impression that she had 'strong leanings' towards Comte's religion of humanity; and Lewes, dissenting from the later, doctrinaire Comte in an article of 1866, admitted that he had 'learned (from the remark of one very dear to me) to regard [the *Politique positive*] as an utopia, presenting hypotheses rather than doctrines, suggestions for future enquirers rather than dogmas for adepts'.

It is clear that George Eliot was generally in agreement with Comte's ideas. In *Romola* in particular she could analyse and, she hoped, 'make incarnate' a past society in which aspects of all three of Comte's stages might be glimpsed. Thus Romola represents the negating, sceptical, 'Renaissance' spirit, which she shares with her learned father, Bardo; she is converted briefly (and regressively) to the fanatical, 'medieval' religious belief of her brother and the great preacher Savonarola; and finally she moves forward into the positivist stage, in which, as a secular 'madonna', she cares for the people of a plague-ridden village. George Eliot was aware of some failures in achieving this scheme artistically. She admitted that she was forced into a 'more ideal treatment of Romola' than she had intended, but insisted that she had always had in mind strong 'romantic and symbolical elements' (L IV 104). Richard Holt Hutton shrewdly commented that Romola herself struck him as 'rather modern', as if she had a knowledge which 'she might have picked up by a study of L. Feuerbach' (letter to George Eliot in 1863). Certainly the attempt to make the 'idea' of Romola 'thoroughly incarnate' is not wholly successful. We scarcely believe in either her religious or her positivist stage of development. We never see her at prayer or confession, nor can we (could George Eliot?) so imagine her. It is not only George Eliot but, awkwardly, Romola herself who seems to see past one phase to the next.

Another comparative failure is the medium of Florentine society in which Romola, Tito and Savonarola move. So intense is George Eliot's desire for historical accuracy and local detail that she crowds her scenes with odd, chatty, colourful characters speaking a dialect she painstakingly reproduces, often with English translations:

'Diavolo!' said Bratti, as he and his companion came, quite unnoticed, upon the noisy scene; 'the Mercato is gone as mad as if the Holy Father had excommunicated us again. I must know what this is. But never fear: it seems a thousand years to you till you see the pretty Tessa, and get your cup of milk; but keep hold of me, and I'll hold to my bargain. Remember, I'm to have the first bid for your suit, specially for the hose, which, with all their stains, are the best *panno di garbo* – as good as ruined, though, with mud and weather stains.' (R 59)

Critics contemporary and modern have complained: 'a magnificent piece of cram' (Leslie Stephen); 'smells of the lamp' (Henry James); 'a monument of excogitation and reconstruction' (Leavis). George Eliot knew she had overdone the learning at the expense of the art, but she felt that 'great, great facts have struggled to find a voice through me, and have only

53

been able to speak brokenly' (to Richard Holt Hutton in 1863, L IV 97).

If she did not quite succeed in combining the modes of psychologically rooted historical realism and symbolic myth, she did manage a fine piece of psychological analysis of the slow moral degeneration of Romola's husband, Tito. Anticipating the two unhappy marriages scrutinised in *Middlemarch*, she shows step by step the painful disillusionment of Romola in her union with the clever, attractive, rootless Greek. Tito, from a passive desire for pleasure and comfort, comes to wish his foster-father Baldassare dead, then refuses to acknowledge him. As the private moral decay proceeds, so Tito's public role expands: the 'grand political and social conditions which made an epoch in the history of Italy' (R 267) provide Tito with an outlet for his ambition; he becomes a double spy. George Eliot expresses in Tito's case her Spinozan belief that, despite the pressure of conditions and the initial absence of evil intention, a man must be held responsible for the evil he does. Her portrayal of Tito is thus complex, even ambivalent. Like Spinoza, she sees human beings obeying natural laws, yet she believes also that they must attempt to transcend those laws:

Our lives make a moral tradition for our individual selves, as the life of mankind at large makes a moral tradition for the race, and to have once acted nobly seems a reason why we should always be noble. But Tito was feeling the effect of an opposite tradition: he had won no memories of self-conquest and perfect faithfulness from which he could have a sense of falling. (R 420)

Tito has failed to do what Spinoza tentatively recommends in the *Ethics*:

The best thing then we can bring to pass, as long as we have no perfect knowledge of our emotions, is to conceive some manner of living aright or certain rules of life, to commit them to memory, and to apply them continuously to the individual things which come in our way frequently in life, so that our imagination may be deeply affected with them and they may be always ready for us.

In denying knowledge of his foster-father, Tito has remained the victim of his passions and has unconsciously opened the way to wrongdoing: 'He hardly knew how the words had come to his lips: there are moments when our passions speak and decide for us, and we seem to stand by and wonder. They carry in them an inspiration of crime, that in one instant does the work of long premeditation' (R 283–4). 'Tito was experiencing that inexorable law of human souls, that we prepare ourselves for sudden deeds by the reiterated choice of good or evil which gradually determines character' (R 287). Though George Eliot writes thus sympathetically of Tito's case, she states also that it was Tito's 'crime towards Baldassare' to have abandoned his ties with him, thus 'uprooting social and personal virtue' (R 552). In one sense, Tito cannot help acting as he does; he is the helpless victim of his selfish emotions. In another, however, he is a moral agent who bears the responsibility for his actions.

Romola was published in the *Cornhill* in fourteen numbers from July 1862 to August 1863, with illustrations by Frederic Leighton. George Eliot insisted on its being published in unusually long extracts so as not to force too rigid a structure on her. She accepted £7,000 instead of the original £10,000 to secure this freedom for herself. Indeed, she very much disliked serialisation ('cutting up') as a method of publishing her works. In 1864 she noted in her journal – as she was to do many times – 'Horrible scepticism about all things – paralyzing my mind. Shall I ever be good for anything again? ever do anything again?' In fact she began reading Spanish history, and by September 1864 was noting that she had begun 'a drama on a subject that has fascinated me'. This was to be, eventually, the dramatic poem *The Spanish Gypsy*, which shows many of the same intellectual preoccupations as *Romola*. But to the relief of her critical and reading public, and of Blackwood, who welcomed her back, her next publication was another novel of English life.

5 Radical-conservative politics and dramatic poetry

As usual, Lewes made the overture to Blackwood, saying, 'It is a novel of English Provincial Life just after the passing of the Reform Bill in '32. I need not say that the political tone is as *dramatic* and *impartial* as her tone has been in all her writings, and that the fact of the story moving amid political scenes which form its background will only render it more interesting to *all* parties' (letter of April 1866). This was Lewes's way of saying that the radicalism of *Felix Holt, The Radical* was of a conservative kind, not offensive even to Tories like Blackwood. A general interest in the subject could be counted on, since Gladstone introduced in 1866 the Second Reform Bill, which, despite the modesty of its aims to extend the franchise and do away with corrupt boroughs, was hotly disputed in Parliament until it was passed in 1867. Blackwood was so enthusiastic about the novel, which he rated even higher than *Adam Bede*, that he wrote to George Eliot, 'I suspect I am a radical of the Felix Holt breed, and so was my father before me.' And though Karl Marx's comments about the 'affectedness' of Felix Holt (in a letter to his wife in 1869) indicate that he had not read the novel, his critical mention of it shows that what he imagined to be George Eliot's kind of radicalism was not attractive to him.

This need hardly surprise us. George Eliot had welcomed the European Revolutions of 1848; sounding almost like Carlyle in his indignant writings about the pampered rich and the wretched poor, she wrote in a letter of March 1848 about the February uprising in Paris:

I have little patience with people who can find time to pity Louis Philippe and his moustachioed sons. Certainly our decayed monarchs should be pensioned off: we should have a hospital for them, or a sort of Zoological Garden, where these worn-out humbugs may be preserved. It is but justice that we should keep them, since we have spoiled them for any honest trade. Let them sit on soft cushions and have their dinner regularly, but for heaven's sake preserve me from sentimentalizing over a pampered old man when the earth has its millions of unfed souls and bodies. (L I 254)

But in social and political matters, as in religious, the bent of her mind was to conserve rather than to destroy. She joins the tradition of English thinkers, from Burke to Coleridge and later Arnold, who took 'radicalism' to mean criticism of tradition, but equally care for all that was good in it; in other words, a concern for the 'roots' of society. Thus she stresses the importance of the past and of cherishing our memory of it. And this is a moral duty not only for individuals – we have seen that characters like Godfrey Cass and Tito Melema deny the claims of their past with disastrous results for their moral integrity – but also for historians, sociologists and politicians. It was for his 'social-political-conservatism' that she admired the social historian Riehl. Indeed, the last sentence of her 1856 article on Riehl contains a metaphor which expresses perfectly the combination in George Eliot, apparent in *Felix Holt* as in all her works, of belief in progress and caution about attempts to move too fast or to deny the importance of the immediate past:

[Riehl] is as far as possible from the folly of supposing that the sun will go backward on the dial, because we put the hands of our clock backward; he only contends against the opposite folly of decreeing that it shall be mid-day, while in fact the sun is only just touching the mountain-tops, and all along the valley men are stumbling in the twilight. (E 299)

It is characteristic of George Eliot that she should portray her radical idealist, Felix Holt, as one who preaches restraint and the pursuance of duties, rather than machine-breaking and rioting, to the unenfranchised working men of Treby Magna. In an interesting twist of the plot she has Felix lead a rioting crowd *away* from the scene in incriminating circumstances which cause him to be prosecuted as the ringleader. In his speeches in the novel, and even more so in the 'Address to Working Men, by Felix Holt' which Blackwood suggested she write for his magazine in defence of the Second Reform Bill of 1867, Felix stresses the 'dependence of men on each other', the need for 'the preservation of order', the danger of fighting exclusively for oneself or one's own class, 'without caring how that tugging will act on the fine widespread network of society in which [one] is fast meshed' (FH 614). Neither the novel nor the 'Address' offers any plan of political *action*, because of George Eliot's rooted belief that changes both do and should take place slowly, by the natural laws of organic development.

As Lewes and Blackwood predicted, *Felix Holt* offended no party. The critics applauded George Eliot's return to the familiar region of provincial English life. Nevertheless, they showed dissatisfaction with the structure of the novel, for as well as following the story of Felix in its connections with Reform in 1832, the novel contains a tragic drama of nemesis in the lives of the landed Transome family, owners of a large but decaying estate. But George Eliot establishes links between the two themes. Harold Transome returns from abroad to take over the estate, but instead of representing his class interest he plans to stand for Parliament as a Radical; meanwhile the estate has fallen into the hands of the unscrupulous lawyer Jermyn, who – and here the private tragedy of Mrs Transome and the public theme of the natural decline of landed interest combine – is Harold's father.

The author's introduction, imagining a coach ride in 1831, just before the passing of the Reform Bill, brilliantly encapsulates the themes, moving easily from the natural history of the area to the people and their private lives and sorrows. 'There is no private life which has not been determined by a wider public life,' says the narrator later in the novel. She makes that clear in her panoramic sweep at the beginning. As in her survey of the history of Shepperton church in 'Amos Barton', of Milby in 'Janet's Repentance', and of St Ogg's in *The Mill on the Floss*, so here she takes a large, half-ironic view of progress:

Five-and-thirty years ago the glory had not yet departed from the old coach-roads; the great roadside inns were still brilliant with well-polished tankards, the smiling glances of pretty barmaids, and the repartees of jocose ostlers; the mail still announced itself by the merry notes of the horn; the hedge-cutter or the rick-thatcher might still know the exact hour by the unfailing yet otherwise meteoric apparition of the peagreen Tally-ho or the yellow Independent; and elderly gentlemen in pony-chaises, quartering nervously to make way for the rolling swinging swiftness, had not ceased to remark that times were finely changed since they used to see the pack-horses and hear the tinkling of their bells on their very highway.

In those days there were pocket boroughs, a Birmingham unrepresented in parliament and compelled to make strong representations out of it, unrepealed corn laws, three-and-sixpenny letters, a brawny and many-breeding pauperism, and other departed evils; but there were some pleasant things too, which have also departed. *Non omnia grandior ætas quæ fugiamus habet*, says the wise goddess: you have not the best of it in all things, O youngsters! the elderly man has his enviable memories, and not the least of them is the memory of a long journey in mid-spring or autumn on the outside of a stage-coach. Posterity may be shot, like a bullet through a tube, by atmospheric pressure from Winchester to Newcastle: that is a fine result to have among our hopes; but the slow old-fashioned way of getting from one end of our country to the other is the better thing to have in the memory. (FH 75)

The 'inexorable process' of progress and decay is linked to the personal story of a single landed family, the Transomes:

How many times in the year, as the coach rolled past the neglected-looking lodges which interrupted the screen of trees, and showed the river winding through a finely-timbered park, had the coachman answered the same questions, or told the same things without being questioned! That? – oh, that was Transome Court, a place there had been a fine sight of lawsuits about. Generations back, the heir of the Transome name had somehow bargained away the estate. (FH 82)

Following an account of the legal intricacies of the estate's ownership and an introduction to the members of the family, George Eliot moves to the tragedy of family relations. The outward and inner fortunes of the Transomes are wedded in the use of the word 'entail' in the following passage:

And such stories often come to be fine in a sense that is not ironical. For there is seldom any wrong-doing which does not carry along with it some downfall of blindly-climbing hopes, some hard entail of suffering, some quickly-satiated desire that survives, with the life in death of old paralytic vice, to see itself cursed by its woeful progeny – some tragic mark of kinship in one brief life to the far-stretching life that went before, and to the life that is to come after, such as has raised the pity and terror of men ever since they began to discern between will and destiny. (FH 83)

It was for her marvellous study of Mrs Transome – disappointed in her beloved son and forced to watch him set about, Oedipus-like, the discovery of a fact it would have been better for him not to know – that Leavis commended George Eliot in his pioneering work to restore her reputation as a great author (*The Great Tradition*, 1948). George Eliot does not succeed in linking her two themes of public progress and personal tragedy all the time. Felix Holt himself is not realised fully as a character rather than an oracle. Indeed, apart from her rendering of Mrs Transome's pain and Harold's complacency and disgust, she fails to give 'felt life' to the 'organisms' in this novel, being perhaps too occupied with rendering the complexities of the political medium. But Leavis was right to insist that it is the work of a great novelist to make a tragedy out of 'moral mediocrity' such as that of the Transomes.

Tragedy had been on George Eliot's mind for some years, and in the work she took up again after *Felix Holt* there was another attempt to combine a tragic theme with the progress of history. Frederic Harrison, a positivist and lawyer who had advised her on the legal plot of *Felix Holt*, wrote her an interesting letter in July 1866. He suggested she write a poetic drama embodying 'the idealization of certain normal [i.e. positivist] relations'. Harrison went on to sketch a possible setting – rural France, where 'the social tone of Catholicism lingers', though not the dogma – and suggest a plot which would include most of Comte's social types: the ruler, the capitalist, the labourer, the physician doing the social duties once performed by the priest, and the mother embodying love and care. George Eliot replied discouragingly of the difficulty of making living art out of such ideas, admitting that she had tried 'to give *some* out of the normal relations' in *Romola*. 'I felt that the necessary idealization could only be attained by adopting the clothing of the past. And again, it is my way, (rather too much so perhaps) to urge the human sanctities through tragedy – through pity and terror as well as admiration and delights' (L IV 301). Still, she hoped she might do something of what Harrison required, if only 'in a fragmentary way'. Then she told him she was taking up an unfinished work, a drama. This was to be the dramatic poem *The Spanish Gypsy* (1868), which embodies tragedy and, in a limited sense because of the tragedy, positivism.

In some notes she wrote on tragedy and *The Spanish Gypsy*, George Eliot took up again the point she had made in her *Antigone* essay that Greek tragedy was founded on the clash of two claims, the 'irreparable collision between the individual and the general (in differing degrees of generality). It is the individual with whom we sympathise, and the general of which we recognise the irresistible power.' Thus Fedalma, engaged to the Spanish Duke Silva, discovers she is the daughter of the gypsy leader, Zarca, who calls on her to renounce her love for Silva and take up her duty as his daughter and a leader of their oppressed people. Although she speaks up, like Stephen Guest, for the ties of affection – 'And that is nature too, /Issuing a fresher law than laws of birth' – she agrees to do her larger duty. Zarca paints the future of his people, once liberated and living in Africa, in positivist terms:

> Oh, it is a faith
> Taught by no priest, but by their beating hearts:
> Faith to each other . . .
>   the fidelity
> Of men whose pulses leap with kindred fire,
> Who in the flash of eyes, the clasp of hands,
> The speech that even in lying tells the truth
> Of heritage inevitable as birth,
> Nay, in the silent bodily presence feel
> The mystic stirring of a common life
> Which makes the many one.

But the positivist vision is not realised. Tragic events, in which Zarca is killed by Silva, intervene. And Fedalma, instead of being the positivist feminine vehicle of fellowship in her community, sees the gypsies fall into arguing factions. Standing on the southern Spanish shore, she sees herself rather 'as the funeral urn that bears /The ashes of a leader'. Tragedy and disappointment displace the optimism of the positivist faith. Here is perhaps the clearest statement of George Eliot's relations with positivism. As a thinker she believed in its version of social progress (though perhaps disagreeing in particulars), but as an artist she often felt compelled to write, as in *The Spanish Gypsy* and *Middlemarch*, tragedy – or something so melancholy as to suggest the possibility of tragedy.

No one reads *The Spanish Gypsy* now, though George Eliot's contemporaries were polite. Blackwood was 'puzzled' by it, wondering 'how far a Poem which requires the reader to pause and dwell so much at every step to feel it aright' could be popular. Henry James saw its 'want of heat, of a quickening central flame'. Reflection, not imagination, had presided at its writing. He could not have known that George Eliot had followed the unpromising course of writing the work in prose, then versifying it. Her verse does not sing. She is tempted into 'Shakespearian' epigrammatical, metaphorical writing; there is scarcely a speech which is not witty or wise or both. Silva and Fedalma converse in parables:

> Don Silva.
> Yes, dearest, it is true.
> Speech is but broken light upon the depth
> Of the unspoken: even your loved words
> Float in the larger meaning of your voice
> As something dimmer.

The work sold surprisingly well, particularly in America. From Cambridge, Massachusetts, George Eliot received an adoring letter from a female admirer – one of many such she was to attract from now on. Mrs Peirce wrote, 'O how wise thou art! Where didst thou learn it all? – Darling, The Spanish Gypsy made me sad, it was so noble: the poetry was so beautiful, but must noble women always fail?' The last question raises an issue on which George Eliot was confessedly divided. Naturally enough, she was approached on all sides by those with an interest in the education, social function and rights of women. She gladly subscribed in 1868 to the founding of Girton College, and wrote to Barbara Bodichon, 'the better Education of Women is one of the objects about which I have *no doubt*'. If Tom Tulliver's schooling had left him unprepared for practical life, Maggie had had very little education of any kind, and was correspondingly bitter. But when Maggie says, 'you are a man, Tom, and have power, and can do something in the world' (MF 450), or when George Eliot says of Esther Lyon in *Felix Holt*, 'after all, she was a woman, and could not make her own lot' (FH 524–5), we are not sure that George Eliot is in complete rebellion against the existing state of things. The *Felix Holt* passage continues, 'Her lot is made for her by the love she accepts,' and our last sight of Esther in the novel is of the faithful wife helping the public man, Felix, and bearing him children. So also at the end of *Middlemarch* Dorothea is to make her mark on society as the wife and helper of Will, now a politician and 'ardent public man'. Though George Eliot welcomed John Stuart Mill's speeches on women's rights and admired his book *On the Subjection of Women* (1869), she was reluctant to support the cause of political equality for women, calling the Women's Suffrage question 'an extremely doubtful good' (letter to Sara Hennell, 1867).

Undoubtedly, her discouraging response to correspondents on the subject has to do with her acute awareness of her own difficult social position. With her yearning to be conventional, she would hardly wish to take up noisily the battle for women. But there is also evidence, in the works and in letters, that as a general philosophy she shared Comte's and Feuerbach's view of the social function of women as primarily that of marrying, bearing children and forging human links with others through their love. To the founder of Girton College, Emily Davies, she wrote in 1868, arguing physiologically and psychologically:

1. The physical and physiological differences between women and men. On the one hand these may be said to lie on the surface and be palpable to every impartial person with common sense who looks at a large assembly made up of both sexes. But on the other hand the differences are deep roots of psychological development, and their influences can be fully traced by careful well-instructed thought. Apart from the question of sex, and only for the sake of illuminating it, take the mode in which some comparatively external physical characteristics such as quality of skin, or relative muscular power among boys, will enter into the determination of the ultimate nature, the *proportion* of feeling and all mental action, in the given individual. This is the deepest and subtlest sort of education that life gives.

2. The spiritual wealth acquired for mankind by the difference of function founded on the other, primary difference; and the preparation that lies in woman's peculiar constitution for a special moral influence. In the face of all wrongs, mistakes, and failures, history has demonstrated that gain. And there lies just that kernel of truth in the vulgar alarm of men lest women should be 'unsexed.' We can no more afford to part with that exquisite type of gentleness, tenderness, possible maternity suffusing a woman's being with affectionateness, which makes what we mean by the feminine character, than we can afford to part with the human love, the mutual subjection of soul between a man and a woman – which is also a growth and revelation beginning before all history. (L IV 467–8)

Though it had been her lot to experience this function of womanhood only partially – she and Lewes had decided not to have children because of their situation – and though she had been able to write, as it were, as a man in her novels, she was none the less unwilling to abandon the traditional position with regard to women. And if it seems surprising that she was not more enthusiastic about the extension of the suffrage to women, we need only remember Felix Holt's 'Address' to see that her doubts applied equally to the extension of the suffrage for men. If in her philosophy George Eliot combined a general optimism with a specific pessimism, in her political views she embraced both approval of radical progress and reluctance to see traditions change.

6 The scientific study of provincial life

Middlemarch, subtitled 'A Study of Provincial Life', addressed itself, among other things, to the question of woman's role in society. Like Fedalma in *The Spanish Gypsy*, though for more complex reasons, Dorothea fails to achieve her noble ideals. In the Prelude George Eliot suggests that Saint Theresa of Avila's life presents an example of a heroic idea occurring in circumstances favourable to its practical embodiment. Saint Theresa 'found her epos in the reform of a religious order'. Not all such women have been so lucky:

Many Theresas have been born who found for themselves no epic life wherein there was a constant unfolding of far-resonant action; perhaps only a life of mistakes, the off-spring of a certain spiritual grandeur ill-matched with the meanness of opportunity: perhaps a tragic failure which found no sacred poet and sank unwept into oblivion. (M 25)

With characteristic complexity of vision, and perhaps even with a certain blurring of distinctions, George Eliot seems to say that such women usually fail because of the uncongenial conditions in which they are fated to live and strive, rather than because of inherent failures of character:

Some have felt that the same blundering lives are due to the inconvenient indefiniteness with which the Supreme Power has fashioned the natures of women: if there were one level of feminine incompetence as strict as the ability to count three and no more, the social lot of women might be treated with scientific certitude. . . . Here and there is born a Saint Theresa, foundress of nothing, whose loving heart-beats and sobs after an unattained goodness tremble off and are dispersed among hindrances, instead of centering in some long-recognizable deed. (M 25–6)

The Finale echoes this melancholy conclusion:

Certainly those determining acts of [Dorothea's] life were not ideally beautiful. They were the mixed result of young and noble impulse struggling amidst the conditions of an imperfect social state, in which great feelings will often take the aspect of error, and great faith the aspect of illusion. . . . A new Theresa will hardly have the opportunity of reforming a conventual life, any more than a new Antigone will spend her heroic piety in daring all for the sake of a brother's burial: the medium in which their ardent deeds took shape is for ever gone. (M 896)

As a consolation, Dorothea is allowed to marry Will Ladislaw, who becomes 'an ardent public man', and she, in helping him, has 'an incalculably diffusive' effect – a beneficent one – on those around her. It is a Comtean solution, but one which is rather negatively embraced: 'Many who knew [Dorothea] thought it a pity that so substantive and rare a creature should have been absorbed into the life of another, and be only known in a certain circle as a wife and mother' (M 894). As one young American reader was reported to have said, on finishing the novel with tears in his eyes: 'My God! and is that all?'

Nowhere is George Eliot's ambivalence more in evidence than here, both on the specific question of what women *should* do and what they *can* do, and on the general issue of which it is a part, namely that of the exact relation of organism to medium, and the possibilities for the individual to act on, and change, society. On the specific question George Eliot has already alerted us to the impossibility of 'scientific certitude' about 'the social lot of women'. Throughout the novel, she gives a masterly analytic presentation of Dorothea in all her mixed internal and external conditions. From the magnificent ironic opening chapters introducing the narrowly educated, Puritan young idealist who thinks 'the really delightful marriage must be that where your husband was a sort of father, and could teach you even Hebrew, if you wished it' (M 32) and who leaps into marriage with the ageing pedant Mr Casaubon on the grounds that it would be like marrying Milton or Pascal, George Eliot shows us, with decreasing irony, Dorothea gaining in breadth of vision and, correspondingly, in imaginative sympathy, at first with her lonely, egotistical husband, and later with Lydgate in his matrimonial and financial troubles. Even at the beginning, where authorial irony surrounds Dorothea, George Eliot reveals with her microscopic lens the narrowness of those who find Dorothea *only* ridiculous. The irony turns deftly in the course of the following paragraph:

And how should Dorothea not marry? – a girl so handsome and with such prospects? Nothing could hinder it but her love of extremes, and her insistence on regulating life according to notions which might cause a wary man to hesitate before he made her an offer, or even might lead her at last to refuse all offers. A young lady of some birth and fortune, who knelt suddenly down on a brick floor by the side of a sick labourer and prayed fervidly as if she thought herself living in the time of the Apostles – who had strange whims of fasting like a Papist, and of sitting up at night to read old theological books! Such a wife might awaken you some fine morning with a new scheme for the application of her income which would interfere with political economy and the keeping of saddle-horses: a man would naturally think twice before he risked himself in such fellowship. Women were expected to have weak opinions; but the great safeguard of society and of domestic life was, that opinions were not acted on. Sane people did what their neighbours did, so that if any lunatics were at large, one might know and avoid them. (M 31)

Authorial irony towards Dorothea has disappeared entirely by the end of the novel. Indeed, in the first published version of the Finale (1871–2) there is a sentence which lays the blame for Dorothea's comparative failure in life squarely at the door of the narrow-minded social medium she inhabits:

Among the many remarks passed on her mistakes, it was never said in the neighbourhood of Middlemarch that such mistakes could not have happened if the society into which she was born had not smiled on propositions of marriage from a sickly man to a girl less than half his own age – on modes of education which make a woman's knowledge another name for motley ignorance – on rules of conduct which are in flat contradiction with its own loudly-asserted beliefs.

This is the only example of a passage removed by George Eliot – as it was for the 1874 *Middlemarch*, on which most subsequent editions have been based – in response to critical outcry. She must have seen the justice of the criticism which reminded her that Dorothea's friends and relations had not 'smiled' on her marriage to Casaubon, but, on the contrary, had pronounced it, in the words of sharp-tongued Mrs Cadwallader, 'as good as going to a nunnery' (M 82). But we may imagine that George Eliot did not recant on the question of the inadequacy of female education. On balance, the sense which remains from the novel, Prelude and revised Finale included, is that in a matter of complex mixed conditions the social medium has proved repressive to the noble, if sometimes mistaken, efforts of the individual.

It might be pointed out to those who saw – and see – in *Middlemarch* chiefly the drama of a woman's failure that the novel is concerned almost equally with the thwarting of a man's efforts by the 'hampering threadlike pressure of small social conditions' in Middlemarch (M 210). Indeed, *Middlemarch* represents the weaving together of two similar but separately conceived stories, that of 'Miss Brooke' and that of Lydgate. Lydgate, the young outsider who comes to Middlemarch professing a strictly scientific medicine – and thus alienating his old-fashioned colleagues of long standing in the community – fails to achieve results in his research into fever and its conditions. George Eliot shows brilliantly how his 'spots of commonness' combine with circumstances to lead him into an unfortunate marriage, and thence into financial debt and a compromising situation in the petty politics of the town. Inner and outer causes combine in an astonishingly tightly woven plot or, as George Eliot puts it, in 'the stealthy convergence of human lots' it is her chosen task to 'study' (M 122). For in *Middlemarch* the familiar role of the narrator as natural historian has been extended, with extraordinary results, to that of the scientific observer. Again and again George Eliot applies the scientific metaphor to her activity. Of Mrs Cadwallader's match-making attempts, for instance, she writes:

Even with a microscope directed on a water-drop we find ourselves making interpretations which turn out to be rather coarse: for whereas under a weak lens you may seem to see a creature exhibiting an active voracity into which other smaller creatures actively play as if they were so many animated tax-pennies, a stronger lens reveals to you certain hairlets which make vortices for these victims while the swallower waits passively at his receipt of custom. In this way, metaphorically speaking, a strong lens applied to Mrs Cadwallader's match-making will show a play of minute causes producing what may be called thought and speech vortices to bring her the sort of food she needed. (M 83)

In her analysis of Lydgate's scientific imagination – like Huxley and Lewes, she stressed the need for imaginative hypotheses, even wrong ones, as well as induction in scientific research – George Eliot might be describing her own process in writing *Middlemarch*, particularly as the analysis concludes with the observation of moral and social, as well as strictly medical, phenomena:

Fever had obscure conditions, and gave [Lydgate] that delightful labour of the imagination which is not mere arbitrariness, but the exercise of disciplined power – combining and constructing with the clearest eye for probabilities and the fullest obedience to knowledge; and then, in yet more energetic alliance with impartial Nature, standing aloof to invent tests by which to try its own work . . . He for his part had tossed away all cheap inventions where ignorance finds itself able and at ease: he was enamoured of that arduous invention which is the very eye of research, provisionally framing its object and correcting it to more and more exactness of relation; he wanted to pierce the obscurity of those minute processes which prepare human misery and joy, those invisible thoroughfares which are the first lurking-places of anguish, mania, and crime, that delicate poise and transition which determine the growth of happy or unhappy consciousness. (M 193–4)

The scientific imagination is akin to the novelist's. George Eliot's ambivalence about the exact cause of Dorothea's or Lydgate's wasted efforts is not inconsistent with her scientific approach to imagined cases. Though she believes in the inexorability of the natural processes she analyses, she is aware that a 'mystery' lies under them (letter of 1859).

Here, as in *The Spanish Gypsy*, she is better able, it seems, to embody the 'positivist' idea in a pessimistic mode. Though Lydgate, like the 'normal' doctor in Harrison's sketch for a positivist novel, reaches out to help the banker Bulstrode whose criminal past has been publicly exposed, and does so 'by that instinct of the Healer which thinks first of bringing rescue or relief to the sufferer' (M 781), it is ironically this very action which finally reduces him in the eyes of the community. The 'petty' social medium is resistant to Lydgate's professional and personal virtues. Yet George Eliot, aware that critics of the novel (as it appeared, in two-monthly parts) called it 'melancholy', wrote to Blackwood in August 1872, assuring him that 'there is no unredeemed tragedy in the solution of the story'. Certainly, Lydgate's ending-up as a fashionable doctor, 'alternating, according to the season, between London and a Continental bathing-place', and the author of a treatise on gout, enduring his disappointing marriage with his 'basil plant' Rosamond, is an unhappy solution. Nevertheless, Dorothea, in her act of imaginative sympathy towards him, divining his marital problems and knowing his loss of reputation because of his connection with Bulstrode, makes him better able to 'accept his narrowed lot with sad resignation. He had chosen this fragile creature, and had taken the burthen of her life upon his arms. He must walk as he could, carrying that burthen pitifully' (M 858). Dorothea herself finally makes a happy second marriage, in which love and duty coincide, and we are told she is able to act beneficently on others. We have seen her, in the course of the novel, undergo a Spinozan education in the extension of her sympathies. She moves through her disillusion with her marriage to Casaubon to a greater 'clearness' of perception about her relation to others – including her husband – in society. Her growing awareness in her life with him is measured by the fact that 'she was no longer struggling against the perception of facts, but adjusting herself to their clearest perception' (M 400). It is Lydgate's tragedy that he, the medical man who is so scrupulous about making the right connections in the pursuit of his scientific researches, does not 'get his mind clear' in his emotional and social life. Thus he is conscious of 'wasted energy and a degrading preoccupation' and of 'a grand existence in thought and effective action lying around him, while his self was being narrowed into the miserable isolation of egoistic fears' (M 697–8).

Imagination is the chief key to moral action in Spinoza's system. Self-interest is unavoidably man's motivating force, but by reflecting on it and thus on the fact that if I am of supreme interest to myself, so also is my fellow man of supreme interest to himself, I can act altruistically: 'By the fact that we imagine a thing which is like ourselves, and which we have not regarded with any emotion, to be affected with any emotion, we are also affected with a like emotion' (*Ethics*). George Eliot's most celebrated expression of the idea comes in chapter twenty-one of *Middlemarch*:

We are all of us born in moral stupidity, taking the world as an udder to feed our supreme selves: Dorothea had early begun to emerge from that stupidity, but yet it had been easier for her to imagine how she would devote herself to Mr. Casaubon, and become wise and strong in his strength and wisdom, than to conceive with that distinctness which is no longer reflection but feeling – an idea wrought back to the directness of sense, like the solidity of objects – that he had an equivalent centre of self, whence the lights and shadows must always fall with a certain difference. (M 243)

Dorothea's sympathy has a 'saving influence' on Lydgate, and her great moral action is her visit to Rosamond to speak on Lydgate's behalf, despite her agonising jealousy of what she wrongly believes to be an affair between Rosamond and Will Ladislaw. The famous chapter eighty-one is headed by a quotation from Goethe's *Faust* relating to the possibility of striving to reach a 'higher' form of life. In Spinozan terms – the language of 'clear ideas', 'reflection', 'pitying fellowship', and 'energy' permeates the chapter – Dorothea acts out of a necessary self-interest wrought into moral action by imaginative sympathy. Dorothea, sexually jealous, reflects: 'Was she alone in that scene? Was it her event only? She forced herself to think of it as bound up with another woman's life' (M 845). She is well able, after her marriage to Casaubon, to sympathise with Lydgate's and Rosamond's unhappiness with one another. She can make an active leap of sympathy for Rosamond, in spite of – even partly because of – her jealousy of her. As a result, Rosamond, by a 'reflex' of Dorothea's effort, makes a sympathetic gesture too, telling Dorothea of her mistake about Will, and indicating that Will loves Dorothea. This action prepares for the scene in which Dorothea and Will declare their love.

Almost all critics of *Middlemarch* have expressed dissatisfaction with Will as a husband for Dorothea. In agreement with Mrs Cadwallader and the others, but not with the author, they think this marriage as much a mistake as the first. It is true that George Eliot fails to render Will Ladislaw with the control with which she manages the other main characters. He never recovers from the descriptions of him by others: 'an Italian with white mice' (Mrs Cadwallader), 'a sort of Daphnis in coat and waistcoat' (Lydgate), nor, conversely, from the too eagerly fond descriptions by the narrator of Will's curls and brightness. The fault lies partly in his rather passive function in the novel. He is 'the one person whom [Dorothea] had found receptive' (M 398), and the plot requires him to be rootless and moneyless and therefore unable to take the initiative in wooing Dorothea. Nevertheless, in spite of what Henry James called an 'elaborate solemnity' in the 'ludicrously excessive' wooing scenes, George Eliot sustains her minute analysis of relationships here as elsewhere in the novel. Like Goethe in *Wilhelm Meister* (which she was reading again while she wrote *Middlemarch*), she dares to present a clichéd, commonplace 'romantic' love scene, in this case one with lightning flashes and claps of thunder sending the lovers into a passionate embrace. Again like Goethe, she dares to be humorous about her hero and heroine. Dorothea, her emotions in turmoil after Rosamond's revelations, is trying to concentrate on the geography of Asia Minor: 'this morning she might make herself finally sure that Paphlagonia was not on the Levantine coast, and fix her total darkness about the Chalybes firmly on the shores of the Euxine' (M 864). When Will arrives, 'he took her hand and raised it to his lips, with something like a sob. But he stood with his hat and gloves in the other hand, and might have done for a portrait of a Royalist.' And the scientific analyst is at work here too. George Eliot notes that the lightning causes Will to take Dorothea's hand 'with a spasmodic movement'. She shows how precarious human relationships are. The interview might have ended in a parting. The weather conditions form part of those minute 'hairlets' of conditions which operate in the progress of relationships.

Indeed, George Eliot's ability to analyse and present as 'felt life' the relationship between two people in marriage is amazing. What Leavis approvingly called her 'hold on dialogue' matches her descriptive power in conveying the pains of the Dorothea–Casaubon and Lydgate–Rosamond relationships. Dialogue and analysis interlock, as in this exchange between Lydgate and his wife on the subject of their falling into debt:

It was evening when he got home. He was intensely miserable, this strong man of nine-and-twenty and of many gifts. He was not saying angrily within himself that he had made a profound mistake; but the mistake was at work in him like a recognised chronic disease, mingling its uneasy importunities with every prospect, and enfeebling every thought. As he went along the passage to the drawing room, he heard the piano and singing. Of course, Ladislaw was there. Lydgate had no objection in general to Ladislaw's coming, but just now he was annoyed that he could not find his hearth free. When he opened the door the two singers went on towards the key-note, raising their eyes and looking at him indeed, but not regarding his entrance as an interruption. To a man galled with his harness as poor Lydgate was, it is not soothing to see two people warbling at him, as he comes in with the sense that the painful day has still pains in store. His face, already paler than usual, took on a scowl as he walked across the room and flung himself into a chair.

The singers feeling themselves excused by the fact that they had had only three bars to sing, now turned round.

'How are you, Lydgate?' said Will, coming forward to shake hands.

Lydgate took his hand, but did not think it necessary to speak.

'Have you dined, Tertius? I expected you much earlier,' said Rosamond, who had already seen that her husband was in a 'horrible humour'. She seated herself in her usual place as she spoke.

'I have dined. I should like some tea, please,' said Lydgate, curtly, still scowling and looking markedly at his legs stretched out before him.

Will was too quick to need more. 'I shall be off,' he said, reaching his hat.

'Tea is coming,' said Rosamond; 'pray don't go.'

'Yes, Lydgate is bored,' said Will, who had more comprehension of Lydgate than Rosamond had, and was not offended by his manner, easily imagining outdoor causes of annoyance.

'There is the more need for you to stay,' said Rosamond, playfully, and in her lightest accent; 'he will not speak to me all the evening.'

'Yes, Rosamond, I shall,' said Lydgate, in his strong baritone. 'I have some serious business to speak to you about.'

No introduction of the business could have been less like that which Lydgate had intended; but her indifferent manner had been too provoking.

'There! you see,' said Will. 'I'm going to the meeting about the Mechanics' Institute. Good-bye'; and he went quickly out of the room.

Rosamond did not look at her husband, but presently rose and took her place before the tea-tray. She was thinking that she had never seen him so disagreeable. Lydgate turned his dark eyes on her and watched her as she delicately handled the tea-service with her taper fingers, and looked at the objects immediately before her with no curve in her face disturbed, and yet with an ineffable protest in her air against all people with unpleasant manners . . . Rosamond said in her silvery neutral way, 'Here is your tea, Tertius,' setting it on the small table by his side, and then moved back to her place without looking at him. Lydgate was too hasty in attributing insensibility to her; after her own fashion, she was sensitive enough, and took lasting impressions. Her impression now was one of offence and repulsion. But then, Rosamond had no scowls and had never raised her voice: she was quite sure that no one could justly find fault with her.

Perhaps Lydgate and she had never felt so far off each other before; but there were strong reasons for not deferring his revelation, even if he had not already begun it by that abrupt announcement; indeed some of the angry desire to rouse her into more sensibility on his account which had prompted him to speak prematurely, still mingled with his pain in the prospect of her pain. But he waited till the tray was gone, the candles were lit, and the evening quiet might be counted on: the interval had left time for repelled tenderness to return into the old course. He spoke kindly.

'Dear Rosy, lay down your work and come to sit by me,' he said, gently, pushing away the table, and stretching out his arm to draw a chair near his own.

Rosamond obeyed. As she came towards him in her drapery of transparent faintly-tinted muslin, her slim yet round figure never looked more graceful; as she sat down by him and laid one hand on the elbow of his chair, at last looking at him and meeting his eyes, her delicate neck and cheek and purely-cut lips never had more of that untarnished beauty which touches us in spring-time and infancy and all sweet freshness. It touched Lydgate now, and mingled the early moments of his love for her with all the other memories which were stirred in this crisis of deep trouble. He laid his ample hand softly on hers, saying –

'Dear!' with the lingering utterance which affection gives to the word. Rosamond too was still under the power of that same past, and her husband was still in part the Lydgate whose approval had stirred delight. She put his hair lightly away from his forehead, then laid her other hand on his, and was conscious of forgiving him.

'I am obliged to tell you what will hurt you, Rosy. But there are things which husband and wife must think of together. I daresay it has occurred to you already that I am short of money.'

Lydgate paused; but Rosamond turned her neck and looked at a vase on the mantlepiece.

'I was not able to pay for all the things we had to get before we were married, and there have been expenses since which I have been obliged to meet. The consequence is, there is a large debt at Brassing – three hundred and eighty pounds – which has been pressing on me a good while, and in fact we are getting deeper every day, for people don't pay me the faster because others want the money. I took pains to keep it from you while you were not well; but now we must think together about it, and you must help me.'

'What can *I* do, Tertius?' said Rosamond, turning her eyes on him again. That little speech of four words, like so many others in all languages, is capable by varied vocal inflexions of expressing all states of mind from helpless dimness to exhaustive argumentative perception, from the completest self-devoting fellowship to the most neutral aloofness. Rosamond's thin utterance threw into the words 'What can *I* do?' as much neutrality as they could hold. They fell like a mortal chill on Lydgate's roused tenderness. (M 636–40)

The mixture of love and loathing between two temperamentally ill-matched but biologically well-matched people is rendered here with a fine combination of general observation and detailed embodiment. The metaphor of a chronic disease to describe the effect of the marriage on Lydgate permeates the passage, explaining his inability to resist rising to anger at Rosamond's indifference and 'neutrality'. Her turning away from him to concentrate on objects at those moments when her participation is most needed, and her 'little speech' refusing to accept her part in their joint troubles are the all too credible particular examples of the 'chronic' nature of the misalliance.

At the same time, George Eliot conveys a painfully real physical attraction between the two, a positive element in their relationship which is immediately undermined by Rosamond's unfortunate 'consciousness' of forgiving Lydgate for his 'horrible humour'.

The novel was published in a new form, eight five-shilling parts at two-monthly intervals, in order to avoid, on the one hand, the four-volume format, which the circulating libraries would not buy, and, on the other, serialisation, which George Eliot disliked. As a result, readers and critics lived with the book as it 'unfolded'. Blackwood enthused over each part as it arrived: 'The mere reading of it has made me think with contempt of lunch, the gong for which is about to sound.' And, 'my wife and daughter have read Book 7 and are in a great state of excitement. They feel ahead of the rest of the world.' Richard Holt Hutton, reviewing each part as it came out, was caught up in its powerful progress:

We all grumble at *Middlemarch*; we all say that the action is slow, that there is too much parade of scientific and especially physiological knowledge in it, that there are turns of phrase which are even pedantic, and that occasionally the bitterness of the commentary on life is almost cynical, but we all read it, and all feel there is nothing to compare with it appearing at the present moment in the way of English literature, and not a few of us calculate whether we shall get the August number before we go for our autumn holiday, or whether we shall have to wait for it till we return.

By the time he came to Book Six, he ventured to write, '*Middlemarch* bids more than fair to be one of the great books of the world.' Henry James, though finding the structure not unified enough, thought that it 'sets a limit to the development of the old-fashioned English novel'. Virginia Woolf's famous comment in 1919 that *Middlemarch* was 'one of the few

English novels written for grown-up people' may be taken alongside Freud's remark that it 'illuminated important aspects of his relations' with his wife. 'My writing', wrote George Eliot to Dr Joseph Payne in 1876, 'is simply a set of experiments in life.' There can be no more eloquent or sophisticated fulfilment of the requirement felt by most readers that literature, particularly. novels, should reflect life than the 'experiment' of *Middlemarch*.

7 A cosmopolitan vision

Daniel Deronda was a new departure. All the previous novels
had been set in the past, and all except *Romola* had dealt
primarily with English provincial life of the lower and middle
classes. George Eliot's last novel is set in the mid-1870s in
which it was written, and widens its panoramic social scope to
include the English gentry, the fashionable watering-places of
Europe, and European Jewry from London to Frankfurt and
Genoa. Furthermore, where previous novels seemed to show
ideals always being hampered and thwarted, in *Daniel Deronda*
George Eliot daringly endorses the visionary Zionist ideals
embraced by Deronda. Her avowed task, against opposition
she expected and got from readers and critics, was to 'widen
the English vision a little' (letter to Blackwood in 1876). She
explained to Harriet Beecher Stowe that her aim was 'to rouse
the imagination of men and women to a vision of human
claims in those races of their fellow-men who most differ from
them in customs and beliefs'. As we might expect, her method
was to stress the fellowship between Christians and Jews,
particularly in terms of their shared religious and cultural
heritage. Daniel Deronda is the link. By engineering the plot
round his upbringing as the 'nephew' of a member of the
English landed class and his gradual discovery of his Jewish
blood and growing interest in the founding of a 'national
centre' in the East to restore 'a political existence to my people'
(DD 875), she has him move between the two worlds, widening
sympathies and forging links.

In order to achieve this, George Eliot makes an experiment with structure. The metaphor of webs, of 'threads of

connection', and their observation by the narrator, operates here as in *Middlemarch*, but the opening of the novel differs from the familiar 'natural history' of her other books. Instead, George Eliot chooses a pregnant moment, immediately before a crisis, to introduce Gwendolen and Deronda and establish a link between them, then traces their past histories up to that moment, before proceeding to give us the crisis itself – Gwendolen's hearing of her family's financial ruin, which predisposes her to accept the morally unacceptable Grand-court as a husband. By this means she makes us privy to the mixed motives operating in Gwendolen when she 'chooses' her husband, at the same time suggesting an even broader canvas for her study of relationships than in her previous works. The scene is a gambling casino in a German spa, where every variety of 'European type' can be found together: 'Livonian and Spanish, Graeco-Italian and miscellaneous German, English aristocratic and English plebeian. Here certainly was a striking admission of human equality' (DD 36). Gambling is not only seen as a class leveller; it acts as a metaphor in the novel for human choice and relationships. Gwendolen gambles on happiness in taking financial security in marriage rather than poor spinsterhood as a governess. Daniel, in his mission, half chosen and half thrust upon him by others who find his influence 'saving', reminds Gwendolen that often, in life as at the tables, 'our gain is another's loss' (DD 383). In the opening scenes Deronda 'redeems' the necklace Gwendolen has pawned; throughout the novel he has a 'redeeming influence' on the lives of friends both Jewish and Gentile.

Critics who have complained of the loose structure of the work, 'cutting' it 'into scraps and talking of nothing in it but Gwendolen', as George Eliot complained to Barbara Bodichon, or, more radically, proposing that the 'good part' of the novel be prised from the mistaken whole and called 'Gwendolen Harleth' (Leavis's famous and influential, though later recanted, suggestion), have not given the structure and imagery their proper attention. It remains true that George Eliot fails to render Daniel and the other Jewish characters with the same minuteness and persuasiveness as Gwendolen, but she succeeds a great deal better in showing the connections between her themes and characters than has usually been admitted. For one thing, we are prepared imperceptibly for a sympathetic response to the revelation of Deronda's Jewishness by the persistent use of appropriate language about him. As a boy he has 'a love of universal history'. In his curiosity about his unknown parentage, his sense of 'an entailed disadvantage' might, we are told, have turned him into 'an Ishmaelite'. Secondly, George Eliot introduces a cultured European Jew, the musician Klesmer (loosely based on Anton Rubinstein, whom she had met in Weimar). Klesmer functions as a critic of the unpleasantly provincial attitude of the English aristocracy in the novel. George Eliot's satire of this society is shrewdly observed social comedy of the best English kind – like Fielding's, Jane Austen's or E.M. Forster's – but it is more. It shows up a negative instance of that 'separateness' of races and classes which, in the Jewish vision of the future in this novel, is to be positively combined with fellowship and 'community'. Here is a scene in the 'magnificent mansion' of a landed family, the Arrowpoints:

Meanwhile enters the expectant peer, Mr Bult, an esteemed party man who, rather neutral in private life, had strong opinions concerning the districts of the Niger, was much at home also in the Brazils, spoke with decision of affairs in the South Seas, was studious of his parliamentary and itinerant speeches, and had the general solidity and suffusive pinkness of a healthy Briton on the central table-land of life. Catherine, aware of a tacit understanding that he was an undeniable husband for an heiress, had nothing to say against him but that he was thoroughly tiresome to her. Mr Bult was amiably confident, and had no idea that his insensibility to counterpoint could ever be reckoned against him. Klesmer he hardly regarded in the light of a serious human being who ought to have a vote; and he did not mind Miss Arrowpoint's addiction to music any more than her probable expenses in antique lace. He was consequently a little amazed at an after-dinner outburst of Klesmer's on the lack of idealism in English politics ... Mr Bult was not surprised that Klesmer's opinions should be flighty, but was astonished at his command of English idiom and his ability to put a point in a way that would have told at a constituents' dinner – to be accounted for probably by his being a Pole, or a Czech, or something of that fermenting sort, in a state of political refugeeism which had obliged him to make a profession of his music; and that evening in the drawing-room he for the first time went up to Klesmer at the piano, Miss Arrowpoint being near, and said –

'I had no idea before that you were a political man.'

Klesmer's only answer was to fold his arms, put out his nether lip, and stare at Mr Bult.

'You must have been used to public speaking. You speak uncommonly well, though I don't agree with you. From what you said about sentiment, I fancy you are a Panslavist.'

'No; my name is Elijah. I am the Wandering Jew,' said Klesmer, flashing a smile at Miss Arrowpoint, and suddenly making a mysterious wind-like rush backwards and forwards on the piano. Mr Bult felt this buffoonery rather offensive and Polish, but – Miss Arrowpoint being there – did not like to move away.

'Herr Klesmer has cosmopolitan ideas,' said Miss Arrowpoint, trying to make the best of the situation. 'He looks forward to a fusion of races.'

'With all my heart,' said Mr Bult, willing to be gracious. 'I was sure he had too much talent to be a mere musician.'

'Ah, sir, you are under some mistake there,' said Klesmer, firing up. 'No man has too much talent to be a musician. Most men have too little. A creative artist is no more a mere musician than a great statesman is a mere politician. We are not ingenious puppets, sir, who live in a box and look out on the world only when it is gaping for amusement. We help to rule the nations and make the age as much as any other public men. We count ourselves on level benches with legislators. And a man who speaks effectively through music is compelled to something more difficult than parliamentary eloquence.' (DD 283-4)

Klesmer's claim for the influence of the artist is one George Eliot might have made for herself. When asked to speak on behalf of women's suffrage in 1878, she declined, insisting that her 'function' was 'that of the *aesthetic*, not the doctrinal teacher – the rousing of the nobler emotions, which makes mankind desire the social right, not the prescribing of special measures' (L VII 44). The terminology echoes that of the article on Riehl of 1856, and indeed George Eliot insisted to an American correspondent in 1876 that 'there has been no change in the point of view from which I regard our life since I wrote my first fiction – the "Scenes of Clerical Life" '. It is important to recognise this continuity in her artistic aims, but also to realise the difference in scope. If she managed the scathing satire of the 'polite pea-shooting' of English dinner-table conversation with assurance, how could she find a mode of representing the claims on her readers of the Jewish idealist Mordecai without falling into sentimentality and lack of specificity?

No amount of research – and of course she learned Hebrew and became, as Lewes said, as 'profoundly versed in Jewish history and literature' as any rabbi – could guarantee that the Jewish elements in the novel would come alive. As in *Romola*, she had to explain so much about an alien culture that she failed to render it convincingly. So, too, with Mordecai the visionary, though she shows much skill in preparing us to accept the extraordinary number of 'coincidences' which happen in connection with him and Deronda. She opens Book Six ('Revelations') with the Aristotelian motto, 'It is a part of probability that many improbable things will happen.' Further, she allows Mordecai's 'inward prophecy' to be fulfilled. Deronda is the 'prefigured friend' whom Mordecai has been expecting to help him fulfil his Jewish ideals, and he appears to Mordecai against the 'golden background' of sunset over the Thames. As if to indicate that she does not *always* allow prophecies to be miraculously fulfilled, George Eliot earlier uses the term 'prefigured stranger' to introduce the morally inert Grandcourt, who has been the object of Gwendolen's mistaken girlish fancies. In the one case she is dealing with vision, in the other with illusion. Irony is appropriate only to the latter.

The problem is most acute in the presentation of Deronda. 'What can be drearier', asks Henry James's Pulcheria in 'Daniel Deronda: A Conversation' (1876), 'than a novel in which the function of the hero – young, handsome, and brilliant – is to give didactic advice, in a proverbial form, to the young, beautiful, and brilliant heroine?' Deronda's is such a difficult character to render in action that George Eliot too often resorts simply to telling us about his 'reflective and diffusive sympathy' and his priestly effect on others. Like Romola, he seems impossibly 'aware' of the moral possibilities for himself, rather like the tadpole which is 'prescient of the future frog'. There is, it is true, some pleasant mild irony at his expense late in the novel, when Deronda feels irked that his friends have no room in their minds for imagining *his* feelings of love, uncertainty, and jealousy. But his 'life' in the novel depends on his relationship with Gwendolen, who is so much more realised than he is that the difference strikes us forcefully.

Gwendolen is the last of those studies, in which George

Eliot excelled, in mixed moral natures acting and acted on by minutely observed social pressures. True to her ambitious extension of fictional possibilities in this novel, George Eliot renders magnificently the ignorant but educable egoistic girl. As much as Maggie or Dorothea, Gwendolen is insufficiently educated for life, particularly for life with a member of the opposite sex. George Eliot includes in her criticism of English society the collusion of its male members in condoning and respecting the secrecy of a man's sexual experience and keeping girls in ignorance of sexual matters. Gwendolen's crisis turns on her discovery of Grandcourt's 'backstairs' relationship with Lydia Glasher, by whom he has four children, and her decision to marry him in spite of it. Without help from her cowed, unhappy mother, she takes on, intending to master him, the 'dark enigma' which is Grandcourt. George Eliot represents Gwendolen's fear of sexuality with precise physiological and pathological observation. Following Feuerbach, she acknowledges the sexual basis of religious enthusiasm in young girls, relating Gwendolen's fits of hysteria and 'spiritual dread' to the same causes. When her cousin Rex courts her, we are told, in a biological metaphor, 'The perception that poor Rex wanted to be tender made her curl up and harden like a sea-anemone at the touch of a finger' (DD 113). Grandcourt's parasite, the 'useful' Lush, creates in her a 'physical antipathy' of 'shuddering annoyance' (DD 158). The chief factor in Grandcourt's negative courtship of her which predisposes her to accept him is, ominously for their married relations, his 'agreeably distant' wooing and his lack of eagerness to touch or kiss her. In one of the most extraordinary 'love scenes' in all fiction George Eliot shows how Gwendolen's 'decision' to accept Grandcourt can only be seen against the background of her spoilt but sheltered girlish upbringing. Gwendolen is a moral agent. Vanity and fear of

poverty play their part in her motivation. Yet we are made to
see how much more complex a set of motives and pressures
make up the event:

anyone seeing them as a picture would have concluded that they were
in some stage of love-making suspense. And certainly the love-
making had begun: she already felt herself being wooed by this silent
man seated at an agreeable distance, with the subtlest atmosphere of
atta of roses and an attention bent wholly on her. And he also
considered himself to be wooing: he was not a man to suppose that his
presence carried no consequences; and he was exactly the man to
feel the utmost piquancy in a girl whom he had not found quite
calculable.

'I was disappointed not to find you at Leubronn,' he began, his
usual broken drawl having just a shade of amorous languor in it. 'The
place was intolerable without you. A mere kennel of a place. Don't
you think so?'

'I can't judge what it would be without myself,' said Gwendolen,
turning her eyes on him, with some recovered sense of mischief.
'With myself I liked it well enough to have stayed longer, if I could.
But I was obliged to come home on account of family troubles' . . .

'Perhaps there is some deeper interest? Some attraction – some
engagement – which it would have been only fair to make me aware
of? Is there any man who stands between us?'

Inwardly the answer framed itself, 'No; but there is a woman.' Yet
how could she utter this? Even if she had not promised that woman to
be silent, it would have been impossible for her to enter on the
subject with Grandcourt. But how could she arrest this wooing by
beginning to make a formal speech – 'I perceive your intention – it is
most flattering, &c.'? A fish honestly invited to come and be eaten has
a clear course in declining, but how if it finds itself swimming against
a net? And apart from the network, would she have dared at once to
say anything decisive? Gwendolen had not time to be clear on that
point. As it was, she felt compelled to silence, and after a pause,
Grandcourt said –

'Am I to understand that some one else is preferred?'

Gwendolen, now impatient of her own embarrassment, determined to rush at the difficulty and free herself. She raised her eyes again and said with something of her former clearness and defiance, 'No' – wishing him to understand, 'What then? I may not be ready to take you.' . . . the subtly-varied drama between man and woman is often such as can hardly be rendered in words put together like dominoes, according to obvious fixed marks. The word of all work Love will no more express the myriad modes of mutual attraction than the word Thought can inform you what is passing through your neighbour's mind. It would be hard to tell on which side – Gwendolen's or Grandcourt's – the influence was more mixed. At that moment his strongest wish was to be completely master of this creature – this piquant combination of maidenliness and mischief: that she knew things which had made her start away from him, spurred him to triumph over that repugnance; and he was believing that he should triumph. And she – ah, piteous equality in the need to dominate! – she was overcome like the thirsty one who is drawn towards the seeming water in the desert, overcome by the suffused sense that here in this man's homage to her lay the rescue from helpless subjection to an oppressive lot . . .

'Do you command me to go?' No familiar spirit could have suggested to him more effective words.

'No,' said Gwendolen. She could not let him go: that negative was a clutch. She seemed to herself to be, after all, only drifted towards the tremendous decision: – but drifting depends on something besides the currents, when the sails have been set beforehand.

'You accept my devotion?' said Grandcourt, holding his hat by his side and looking straight into her eyes, without other movement. Their eyes meeting in that way seemed to allow any length of pause; but wait as long as she would, how could she contradict herself? What had she detained him for? He had shut out any explanation.

'Yes,' came as gravely from Gwendolen's lips as if she had been answering her name in a court of justice. He received it gravely, and they still looked at each other in the same attitude. Was there ever before such a way of accepting the bliss-giving 'Yes'? (DD 344–8)

Thus Gwendolen 'makes her choice' of Grandcourt, the only main character in all George Eliot's fiction who is represented as morally irredeemable.

In her handling of Deronda's relationship with Gwendolen, George Eliot again strikes an ambitious experimental note. Having established an attraction between them in the first scene in the novel – the opening words, 'Was she beautiful or not beautiful?', record Daniel's thoughts about her as he watches her gamble – she documents minutely the effect each has on the other when they meet later in England. All their meetings take place furtively and interruptedly, in snatched conversations at pianos, in corners, hidden in recesses, and are interpreted, not unreasonably, by Grandcourt as the signs of an adulterous affair. Again George Eliot is demonstrating the complex play of mixed conditions in human relationships. Deronda is, in fact, preaching renunciation and patience to Gwendolen in these illicit conversations, yet his attraction to her, and hers to him, is expressed too. In fact, though love and duty coincide perhaps too neatly for Deronda in his threefold discovery of the Jewish Mirah's love for him, his own Jewishness and his vocation, which Mirah, as Mordecai's sister, is best fitted to share with him, George Eliot insists that his rejection of Gwendolen is nevertheless a renunciation. For he has loved her too, and might view a permanent relationship with her as an alternative duty. 'Love and duty had thrown other bonds around him,' so that the 'impulse' to 'carry out to the last the rescue he had begun in that monitory redemption of the necklace' could 'no longer determine his life' (DD 835). Like Goethe, who shows how Wilhelm Meister's renunciation in love is not an unmixedly heroic action, George Eliot lets inclination and duty coincide in Deronda's relation to Mirah while indicating the complexity of the threads of connection which bind human beings to each other by stressing both his and Gwendolen's loss in the severance of *their* relationship.

When one considers the breath-taking scope of George Eliot's imaginative effort in *Daniel Deronda*, one must concur, not with Robert Louis Stevenson's easy label for Deronda – 'the Prince of Prigs' – or Leavis's drastic prescription for salvaging the 'readable' part of the book, or James's merriment at 'Deronda wiping Gwendolen's tears and Gwendolen wiping his', but with the comment of her faithful publisher Blackwood. Not liking certain parts of the book any more than later readers would, he nevertheless wrote to his London manager Langford, 'she is so great a giant that there is nothing for it but to accept her inspirations and leave criticism alone'. No wonder she wrote in her journal in December 1877, 'Many conceptions of works to be carried out present themselves, but confidence in my own fitness to complete them worthily is all the more wanting because it is reasonable to argue that I must have already done my best' (L VI 440).

Epilogue

In spite of her insistence on her role as an '*aesthetic* teacher', George Eliot was persuaded by the adoration expressed by some self-elected young 'disciples' to depart from fiction. Alexander Main, referred to by the amused Blackwood as 'the Gusher', asked if he might extract passages from her books for a volume called *Wise, Witty, and Tender Sayings*. Though she was aware that such extracting would be damaging to the artistic structure of her works, which she thought not separable into 'direct' and 'indirect' teaching, her self-distrust and love of approbation (noted twenty years before by Combe) induced her to permit it. More than that, she herself produced a volume called *Impressions of Theophrastus Such* in 1878. Blackwood was polite about this set of heavy, moralising sayings: 'It brings us all in a kind of a way to the Confessional.' He could not be other than kind to her, for Lewes had died in November 1878. George Eliot, as it were in imitation of her fictional creation Dorothea, set herself the 'sacred task' of finishing Lewes's last scientific work, *Problems of Life and Mind*. She also agreed to marry, in 1880, John Cross, a man twenty years younger than herself. By so doing she set tongues wagging a second time. One thinks again of Dorothea. Free-thinkers were disappointed in the return to convention; Comtists were offended by her breaking of the principle of eternal widowhood; the orthodox approved, but muttered about the age difference. Her brother Isaac broke his long silence with a stiff letter of 'sincere congratulations' which brought from her a disproportionate expression of gratitude: 'it was a great joy to me to have your kind words of sympathy, for our long silence has never broken that affection for you which began when we were little ones' (L VII 287). She died in December 1880, and John Cross wrote the life of her of which Gladstone announced, 'it is a Reticence in three volumes'.

The *Life* stressed George Eliot's didactic and moral qualities of personality and genius, suppressing examples of her humour and unorthodox candour. This, in combination with *Theophrastus Such* and the increasing tendency in her novels to preface each chapter with a philosophical or literary motto, led to a view of George Eliot as a humourless sibyl. Her reputation plummeted in the years immediately following her death. Trollope felt himself 'in company with some philosopher rather than with a novelist'. W. E. Henley objected facetiously in 1890 to 'the Novel-with-a-Purpose'; he characterised George Eliot as 'George Sand *plus* Science and *minus* Sex' and 'Pallas with prejudices and a corset'. Though Lord David Cecil, writing in 1935, could appreciate her power of analysing 'the moral battle-field', he also called her a 'Philistine'. If Virginia Woolf's short essay of 1919 (reprinted in 1925) perhaps began the work of restoring George Eliot's reputation, it was F. R. Leavis who drew attention boldly to her claim to rank with the great novelists, English and European, in his influential work *The Great Tradition* (1948).

One thing to which Leavis drew timely attention was the lack of 'the atmosphere of the taboo' surrounding sexual matters in her novels. He instanced the sympathetic, no-nonsense treatment of Mrs Transome's affair with Jermyn in *Felix Holt*. One could multiply the cases. It is, remarkably, still an assumption made by many critics that George Eliot was reticent about sex. Yet every work she wrote contains sexual relationships which are in some way 'irregular': Arthur's seduction of Hetty, Maggie's near-elopement with Stephen, Tito's pretend-marriage to Tessa, Will Ladislaw's love for

Dorothea and Rosamond's flirtation with Will, Grandcourt's relationship with Mrs Glasher and, most daringly, Deronda's as-it-were adulterous affair with Gwendolen. It cannot be stressed too much that George Eliot, far from being the most 'Victorian' of Victorian novelists in the presentation of – or the failure to present – sexual relationships, is much more open on the subject than Dickens, Thackeray or even Trollope. Sexuality was a subject she handled unsensationally and uncoyly, as an integral part of the lives of individuals. Victorian critics, perhaps sensing this, rarely complained about George Eliot's openness in sexual matters, except in relation to Hetty and Maggie. That they accepted it in the later novels is a tribute to her non-sensational, scrupulously scientific handling of the subject. George Eliot viewed sexuality in the light of those unalterable 'natural laws' which she believed governed all human affairs, and in her role as artistic analyst studied the physiological as well as moral conditions of her characters. If a theory of art can be deduced from George Eliot's writings, it includes a view of the creative imagination as linked to the imaginative activity of the observing scientist.

On the other hand, there is no doubt that George Eliot's aim was not merely to observe, but also to teach morality. Much adverse criticism of her work, starting with Henry James, has called attention to the 'battle' in her between the artist and the moralist. From the first her view of art was that it should teach, but she hoped, as she wrote of *Middlemarch*, that she had succeeded in making 'matter and form an inseparable truthfulness'. In spite of some sibylline intrusions in her novels, she manages on the whole to achieve the blend. Her ability to analyse character minutely and also show it in action combines with a large intelligence capable of expressing itself in metaphors from an astounding variety of sources. Her ear for the spoken word, particularly in its revelation of humorous inconsistency – one thinks of Dorothea's uncle, Mr Brooke – gave her that 'hold on dialogue' which Leavis praised. Hardy's rustics owe much to hers; Henry James's *Portrait of a Lady* was deeply influenced by *Daniel Deronda* in its portrayal of wooing and marriage; Proust admired her ability to show character in action. Rivalling Jane Austen in the humorous presentation of social manners, she went far beyond her into the detailed presentation of the progress of character and its interaction with society. There are some passages of heavy wisdom taken too far; George Eliot confessed to Blackwood while writing *Middlemarch* that 'I am in danger . . . of parodying dear Goldsmith's satire on Burke, and think of refining when novel readers only think of skipping' (L V 169). Occasionally she sins against her own canon of avoiding idealisation of beautiful heroines and noble heroes ('Silly Novels by Lady Novelists'). Maggie, Romola and Dorothea are beautiful, 'ardent', even sometimes 'adorable'. But on the whole they too are represented as 'mixed and erring human nature'. Her dissection of shades of moral greyness in men like Harold Transome and Bulstrode is unsparing yet not destructive.

Critics complained of her novels' lack of unified structure. Sometimes, it is true, her plotting is over-elaborate. The legal network in *Felix Holt*, the tortuous machinery of Bulstrode's exposure in *Middlemarch*, the Jewish connections in *Daniel Deronda* are examples. But these are mechanical plot aspects. In the inner plotting of Spinozan education of character, of the 'religion of humanity' operating between individuals within the larger social group, George Eliot shows a remarkably tight grasp. Everywhere she demonstrates 'threads of connection' in the societies she creates and analyses. In doing so she follows the difficult philosophy she had embraced ever since her defection from Christianity. She offers a definition of her meliorism in a letter of 1868:

Never to beat and bruise one's wings against the inevitable but to throw the whole force of one's soul towards the achievement of some possible better, is the brief heading that need never be changed, however often the chapter of more special rules may have to be re-written. (L IV 499)

Like Dickens, Tennyson and Hardy, but more consciously and articulately than they, George Eliot responded ambivalently to the intellectual movements and discoveries of her age. She wanted to accept Comte's optimism about the future of a secular society freed from religious and metaphysical creeds, yet, as an artist imagining the lot of the individual in society, what she saw and rendered were the personal tragedies and dislocations of those caught up unconsciously in the onward march of progress. Darwin's evolutionary theory satisfied her intellectual scepticism of supernatural beliefs and plausibly explained the origin and progress of animal and human species, yet she was disturbed at the implications for such 'emmetlike' creatures as the Dodsons and the Tullivers. Strauss demonstrated to her satisfaction the mythical origin of Biblical events, but she celebrated with warmth as well as irony the importance in the lives of ordinary people of a traditional religious creed. Spinoza and Feuerbach among philosophers, and Goethe and Scott among creative writers, most earned her respect by their humane interest in how men are affected by momentous changes and by their tolerance of that clinging to old ways which Marx, for example, despised. And, like Goethe and Scott, she was an artist. Her novels are informed by philosophical concerns, and it is important to understand these, but her medium was art. At her best, she combines the two – philosophy and art – perfectly. How can we separate in our analysis of, say, the relationship of Lydgate and Rosamond the historical, scientific and philosophical observation of the narrator from the achieved imagined existence of the fictional couple? Here George Eliot succeeds magnificently in the avowed task of 'making ideas incarnate'.

Frederic Myers, who told the most famous anecdote of all about George Eliot – pronouncing of God, Immortality and Duty how inconceivable the first, how unbelievable the second, how peremptory and absolute the third – wrote in response to *Middlemarch*:

Life has come to such a pass, – now that there is no longer any God or any hereafter or anything in particular to aim at, – that it is only by coming into contact with some other person that one can be oneself . . . And therefore it is that to read of Dorothea's night of struggle and visit to Rosamond is better, though it is only on paper and in a book, than an ordinary passion; for this is what one wants, though it be but a shadow; this is the best conception of life that in this stage of the world we can form. Scenes like these go straight into the only imperishable world, – the world which is peopled by the lovely conceptions which have disengaged themselves in successive generations from the brains of men. The interest of such conceptions is more than artistic; they are landmarks in the history of the race, showing the height to which, at successive periods, man's ideal of his own life has vision.

And you seem now to be the only person who can make life appear potentially noble and interesting without starting from any assumptions. (L IX 67–8)

The rhetoric is earnest, Victorian. But many a modern reader of *Middlemarch*, too, can say that the reading of it made an epoch in his life.

Further reading

All George Eliot's novels are available in annotated Penguin editions. The standard modern edition is the Clarendon Edition of the Novels of George Eliot, now in progress under the general editorship of Gordon S. Haight. For *Impressions of Theophrastus Such, The Spanish Gypsy* and George Eliot's minor prose and verse, readers should consult the Cabinet Edition of her works, published in twenty volumes (Edinburgh and London, 1878–80). Most of her essays have been collected in Thomas Pinney's helpful volume, *Essays of George Eliot* (London, 1963). Gordon S. Haight's nine-volume edition of the letters (New Haven and London, 1954–6 and 1978) is a model of helpful scholarship. His *George Eliot: A Biography* (Oxford, 1968) is the standard modern biography of George Eliot, though Ruby V. Redinger's psychoanalytical biography, *George Eliot: The Emergent Self* (London, 1975), is also of interest. Most of the quotations in the present work from contemporary critics of George Eliot come from one of two useful collections: *George Eliot: The Critical Heritage* (London, 1971), edited with an excellent introduction by David Carroll and *A Century of George Eliot Criticism*, edited by Gordon S. Haight (London, 1966).

F. R. Leavis's *The Great Tradition* (London, 1948) re-established George Eliot's good name, and Basil Willey's essay on her in *Nineteenth-Century Studies* (London, 1949) placed her in the intellectual climate of the mid-nineteenth century. Barbara Hardy's *The Novels of George Eliot* (London, 1959) and W. J. Harvey's *The Art of George Eliot* (London, 1961) may be recommended for their criticism of the novels. Works on the intellectual background to George Eliot's writings include Bernard J. Paris, *Experiments in Life: George Eliot's Quest for Values* (Detroit, Michigan, 1965), U. C. Knoepflmacher, *Religious Humanism and the Victorian Novel* (Princeton, New Jersey, 1965) and Rosemary Ashton, *The German*

*Idea: Four English Writers and the Reception of German Thought,
1800–1860* (Cambridge, 1980). An excellent article on her philosophy
is George Levine's 'Determinism and Responsibility in the Works of
George Eliot', *Publications of the Modern Language Association of
America*, 77 (1962), 268–79.

Andrew Sanders's *The Victorian Historical Novel, 1840–1880*
(London, 1979) contains an interesting account of *Romola*; Jerome
Beaty's *'Middlemarch' from Notebook to Novel* (Urbana, Illinois,
1960) traces the writing of *Middlemarch* and its complex plotting; J.
A. Sutherland has a chapter on the publication of *Middlemarch* in his
Victorian Novelists and Publishers (London, 1976). Finally, E. S.
Shaffer's *'Kubla Khan' and The Fall of Jerusalem* (Cambridge, 1975)
has an interesting account of *Daniel Deronda* in the context of
German biblical criticism.

References in the present work to philosophical works are taken
from the following editions: David Friedrich Strauss, *The Life of
Jesus* [trans. George Eliot], 3 vols. (London, 1846); Ludwig
Feuerbach, *The Essence of Christianity* [trans. George Eliot]
(London, 1854, reprinted New York, 1957); and Benedict de
Spinoza, *Ethics*, trans. A. Boyle (London, 1948).

Index

Index